EARTH AND SPACE

This book was created by
David West 🏃 Children's Books

ISBN 0-7607-3424-0

Printed in China

Designers
Aarti Parmar
Rob Shone
Fiona Thorne
Illustrators
John Butler
Jim Eldridge
James Field
Andrew & Angela Harland
Colin Howard
Rob Jakeway
Mike Lacey
Sarah Lees
Gilly Marklew
Dud Moseley
Terry Riley
Sarah Smith
Stephen Sweet
Mike Taylor
Ross Watton
(SGA)
Ian Thompson
Cartoonist
Peter Wilks
(SGA)
Editor
James Pickering
Consultant
Steve Parker

EARTH AND SPACE

Written by
Anita Ganeri, John Malam,
Clare Oliver and Adam Hibbert

BARNES
& NOBLE
BOOKS
NEW YORK

CONTENTS

96 Could time stand still?

97 Is time travel possible?

98 Is there anybody out there?

98 How will we find out?

99 Do aliens know about us?

CHAPTER FOUR
LOOKING AT THE
NIGHT SKY

102 Who gazes at the stars?

103 Can anyone be an astronomer?

103 Can you only see the Moon and stars at night?

104 Who built a tomb for the Sun god?

104 Who built a stone circle for the Sun?

105 Who thought the sky was a goddess?

106 Who first wrote about the stars?

107 How do we know about the first astronomers?

107 What was a Babylonian year like?

108 Who thought the Sun was as wide as a ruler?

109 Who named groups of stars?

109 Who worked out the Earth is round?

110 Why do stars make patterns?

110 What is the zodiac?

111 Which stars make a hunter?

112 How did sailors know where they were going?

113 How did an astrolabe work?

113 What is the pole star?

114 Who made the first telescope?

115 How does a telescope work?

115 Who put mirrors in a telescope?

116 Who said that planets go round the Sun?

116 Who was put on trial for star-gazing?

117 Who first used a telescope for astronomy?

118 Where do astronomers put their telescopes?

118 Where's the best place to build an observatory?

119 How can a telescope see through the roof?

120 How deep is space?

120 Are there candles in space?

121 How do you measure the distance to a star?

122 Who made the first radio telescope?

122 Which are the most powerful radio telescopes?

123 Where is the biggest radio telescope?

124 What's a gravity telescope?

124 Can we see black holes?

125 What's the weirdest telescope?

126 Are there telescopes in space?

126 Are there observatories in space?

127 Which telescope is in orbit?

128 What's better than a powerful telescope?

129 Could we build Very Large Arrays in space?

129 Could we build an observatory on the Moon?

CHAPTER FIVE
PREHISTORIC LIFE
ON EARTH

132 How old is the Earth?

132 Has there always been life on the Earth?

133 Has the Earth always looked the same?

134 When and where did life on Earth begin?

135 How did life begin?

135 What were the first living things?

136 What animals lived in the sea?

179 How high are waterfalls?

180 Which lake is the biggest?

181 Where is the highest lake?

181 How are lakes made?

182 What is a coral island?

182 Where is the biggest island?

183 Which country has most islands?

184 Why are deserts dry?

184 Can sand dunes move?

185 Are all deserts sandy?

186 Why are rainforests so wet?

187 Where does the biggest forest grow?

187 How do rainforests grow?

188 What are grasslands?

189 Why did a grassland turn to dust?

189 What are grasslands used for?

**CHAPTER SEVEN
VIOLENT EARTH**

192 Why do volcanoes blow their tops?

193 What is lava?

193 What happened to Pompeii?

194 How long do volcanoes sleep for?

195 Why do people live near volcanoes?

195 Why do geysers gush?

196 What makes the Earth shake?

196 How much damage do earthquakes cause?

197 How do scientists measure an earthquake?

198 What is a tsunami?

199 How do tsunamis start?

199 What happens when a tsunami hits land?

200 How do floods happen?

201 What are flash floods?

201 Are some floods useful?

202 When do thunderstorms happen?

202 What makes thunder rumble?

203 Where do thunderstorms begin?

204 What makes lightning flash?

204 Does lightning ever strike twice?

205 What is ball lightning?

206 Where do avalanches strike?

206 Can people survive avalanches?

207 What sets off an avalanche?

208 Why are blizzards dangerous?

208 Which is the snowiest place?

209 What is a hailstone made from?

210 What are hurricanes?

211 How big are hurricanes?

211 Do hurricanes have eyes?

212 What makes a tornado twist?

213 How quickly do tornadoes travel?

213 Do tornadoes happen at sea?

214 How do wildfires start?

215 How do people fight wildfires?

215 What is a heatwave?

216 What makes the land slide?

216 Where was the worst mudslide?

217 Why do cliffs collapse?

218 What is El Niño?

219 What are monsoons?

219 What is a sandstorm?

CHAPTER EIGHT
OUR EARTH

CHAPTER ONE

OUR SOLAR SYSTEM

? What is the Solar System?

Solar means "of the Sun." The Solar System is centered around the Sun, the shining ball in the sky. It includes the family of nine planets orbiting (traveling around) the Sun, as well as the moons of these planets, and smaller objects, such as comets, asteroids, and bits of space rock. The powerful pull of an invisible force called gravity from the Sun stops these bodies from flying off into deepest space.

Saturn
Distance from Sun
885 million miles
Diameter
80,389 miles

Mars
Distance from Sun
141 million miles
Diameter
4,214 miles

Jupiter
Distance from Sun
482 million miles
Diameter
88,650 miles

Earth
Distance from Sun
93 million miles
Diameter
7,909 miles

Mercury
Distance from Sun
36 million miles
Diameter
3,024 miles

Venus
Distance from Sun
67 million miles
Diameter
7,504 miles

Uranus
Distance from Sun
1,179 million miles
Diameter
31,693 miles

Neptune
Distance from Sun
2,788 million miles
Diameter
30,710 miles

Pluto
Distance from Sun
3,658 million miles
Diameter
1,463 miles

Is it true?
All planets have one moon.

No. Our planet Earth has one moon, called the Moon. But many of the planets have more than one. Our neighbour Mars, for instance, has two! Only the two planets closest to the Sun – Mercury and Venus – have no moons at all.

Amazing! Saturn's not the only planet with rings. Saturn's rings are the easiest to see, but Jupiter, Neptune and Uranus have them, too. Saturn has seven main rings, and then hundreds of thinner rings, called ringlets.

13

How hot is the Sun?

In deserts here on Earth, heat that has traveled 93 million miles from the Sun can be hot enough to fry an egg. The Sun's surface is a super-hot 6,000°C, and its center or core is even hotter.

6,000°C

1,000,000°C

14,000,000°C

Amazing! The Sun is a star – a gigantic ball of burning gas. It has been shining for about five billion years.

14

Why must you never look at the Sun?

Not even sunglasses fully protect your eyes from the Sun's dangerous ultraviolet (UV) rays. UV can burn your eyes and make you blind. If you want to see the Sun safely, ask an adult to show you how to project its image on to a sheet of paper.

Is it true?
The Sun has spots.

Yes. The Sun is not the same color all over. Some areas of its surface are darker. These spots are little pockets that are slightly cooler. Of course, sunspots are only "little" compared to the Sun – some grow to be as large as Jupiter, the biggest planet in the Solar System!

WARNING!
NEVER LOOK AT THE SUN, EVEN IF YOU'RE WEARING SUNGLASSES.

Total eclipse of the Sun

When does the Sun go out?

When there's a total eclipse. This happens when the Moon's path takes it between the Earth and the Sun, and the Moon casts a shadow across the surface of the Earth.

What does Mercury look like?

Planet Mercury looks very like our Moon. It's about the same size and it's covered in craters, where bits of space rock have crash-landed on its surface. The biggest crater is the Caloris Basin, which is about 800 miles across. Mercury also has huge plains, rolling hills, deep gorges, chasms, and cliffs.

Earth

Mercury

Is it true?
Mercury is the smallest planet.

No. Mercury is only about a third the size of the Earth, but Pluto is even smaller. If you could put them on a scale, it would take 21 Plutos to balance one Mercury.

16

The surface of Mercury is covered with craters.

? Is Mercury the hottest planet?

Mercury is the planet closest to the Sun, but its neighbor Venus is even hotter, because it has clouds to keep in the heat.

The surface of Mercury is 350°C during the day, and minus 170°C at night.

? What is the weather like on Mercury?

Mercury doesn't have any weather, because it has no air and hardly any atmosphere. That means there are no clouds to shield the surface of the planet from the baking-hot Sun during the day, or to keep in the heat at night. There is no wind or rain on Mercury, either.

Amazing!.Mercury is the fastest planet. Mercury zooms around the Sun in just 88 days, at an incredible 107,000 mph. That makes it faster than any space rocket ever invented.

17

The planet Venus seen close to the Moon

? When is a star not a star?

When it's a planet! Venus is sometimes called the "evening star" because it's so bright it's one of the first points of light we see shining as it gets dark. Planets don't make their own light – they reflect the Sun's light.

Is it true?
Venus is bigger than the Earth.

No. Venus is a fraction smaller than the Earth, but not by much. Venus is 7,504 miles across, whereas Earth is 405 miles wider. Venus's mass is about four-fifths of Earth's.

Earth

Venus

18

? How can a day be longer than a year?

A day is the amount of time a planet takes to spin on its axis, and a year is the time it takes to travel around the Sun. Venus spins on its axis very slowly, but orbits the Sun more quickly than Earth. A day on Venus lasts 243 Earth-days, but a year is only 225 Earth-days.

Volcanic eruption on Venus

19

? What's special about our planet?

As far as we know, Earth is the only planet in the Solar System that has life.

As well as warmth from the Sun, the other main ingredient for life is liquid water. Earth has plenty of water – in total, it covers about three-quarters of the planet's surface!

 Is it true?
There was life on Earth from the start.

No. When Earth first formed it was extremely hot and there was no oxygen. Over millions of years, the planet cooled, oceans formed and oxygen was made. The first life on Earth appeared about 3 billion years ago.

Earth seen from space

What does Earth look like from space?

It looks beautiful – blue with swirling white clouds. Astronauts in space spend most of their free time gazing at it. They can even make out cities, when they are lit up at night with twinkling lights.

Amazing!
The Earth is magnetic. At the center of the Earth is a core of a molten metal called iron, which makes our planet like a giant magnet. This is what pulls the needle on a compass towards the magnetic North Pole.

Why does our sky go dark at night?

Like all planets, the Earth is spinning as it orbits the Sun. When your part of the planet is facing away from the Sun, its light is blocked out. At the same time, it is daytime for people on the opposite side of the Earth.

? Why does the Moon have so many craters?

Because it has been pelted by so many space rocks and has no atmosphere to protect it. One of the biggest craters, called Bailly, is nearly 190 miles across. You can make out some of the craters using a good pair of binoculars.

Meteorite hitting the Moon

New Moon

Crescent Moon

First quarter Moon

Gibbous Moon

? Why does the Moon change shape?

It doesn't really – it's ball-shaped just like the Earth, but as the Moon travels around the Earth, you see different amounts of its sunlit half. It seems to change gradually from a crescent to a disc, and back again.

Amazing! You can jump higher on the Moon. The Moon's gravity is much weaker than Earth's. This means you would only weigh about a sixth of your Earth-weight there – and you'd be able to jump six times higher!

Full Moon

What is the dark side of the Moon?

It's the part of the Moon that we can never see from Earth. The Moon takes the same time to orbit the Earth as it does to spin once. This means the same side of the Moon always faces away from the Earth.

Is it true?
There are seas on the Moon.

Yes and no. There are dark, rocky plains and craters called maria (Latin for "seas"), but they don't contain water. The first astronauts to visit the Moon landed on the Sea of Tranquillity.

Earth

Mars

Which is the red planet?

Mars was named after the Roman god of war, because of its blood-red color. The planet looks rusty red because its surface is covered with iron-rich soil and rock. There are no seas on Mars, and it is very cold.

Does Mars have ice at its poles?

Yes. Its south pole is mostly "dry ice," which is frozen carbon dioxide gas. At the north pole there may be frozen water, mixed with the frozen carbon dioxide. There may be frozen water underground on Mars, too.

One of Mars's polar caps, at the bottom of the planet

Is it true?

There is life on Mars.

No. Or at least, there's no sure sign of any. But long ago, Mars had flowing rivers of water, so there could have been life once, and there may be fossils buried underground.

What are Mars's moons like?

Mars's two tiny moons, Deimos and Phobos, are not round like our Moon. They look more like baked potatoes! They might have been asteroids (space rocks) that Mars captured with its gravity.

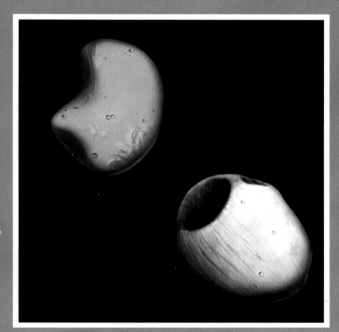

Phobos
(about 9 miles long)

Deimos
(about 17 miles long)

Amazing! There's a record-breaking volcano on Mars. Olympus Mons is about 370 miles across and towers over 15 miles high. It's the Solar System's biggest volcano. Long ago it spurted out runny rivers of black lava.

The Martian surface, showing Olympus Mons

? Which is the biggest planet?

Jupiter is so big that all the other planets in the Solar System could fit inside it! If it was any bigger it might become too hot in the middle, start to glow and turn into another Sun.

Is it true?
Jupiter's striped.

Yes. The planet looks like it's wearing a giant pair of pajamas, because of its bands of cloud. They're made of frozen crystals of water, ammonia and other chemicals.

? What is Jupiter made of?

Jupiter is one of the planets known as the gas giants. About 90 per cent of it is made of gases called hydrogen and helium. At the centre of Jupiter is a small, rocky core, about as big as the Earth.

Core

Gases

Amazing! You could fit two Earths inside the Great Red Spot, which is about 25,000 miles across.

Jupiter

Earth

Where is the storm that never stops?

Violent winds whip up storms all over the planet Jupiter, but the Great Red Spot is the largest. It has been raging away for over 300 years!

The Great Red Spot is a giant storm on Jupiter.

Looking at Jupiter from Io

Which world has most volcanoes?

Jupiter's closest moon, Io, is orange and yellow, because of the sulphur from all its active volcanoes. If you could survive the intense heat, you'd realise that Io smells of rotten eggs!

Which moon is bigger than a planet?

Jupiter's moon Ganymede is the largest moon in the Solar System. At 3,271 miles across, it is bigger than Mercury! Another of Jupiter's moons, Callisto, is a similar size to Mercury.

Ganymede

Looking at Jupiter from Ganymede

Io

Europa

? Which moon might have life?

Jupiter's moon Europa is covered by a thick crust of ice. The ice looks smooth, like frozen water, but it also has lots of cracks. Scientists think there is a liquid ocean beneath the ice – and where there's water, there might be life!

Amazing! Callisto is the most cratered world in the Solar System. Almost every bit of this moon is covered in craters. The biggest one is about 185 miles across. It is called Valhalla, after the place where the Vikings thought brave warriors went when they died.

Callisto

 Is it true?
Jupiter only has four moons.

No. Galileo discovered the four biggest – Callisto, Ganymede, Europa and Io – in 1610. Since then, astronomers have discovered 13 smaller moons as well, making a total of 17.

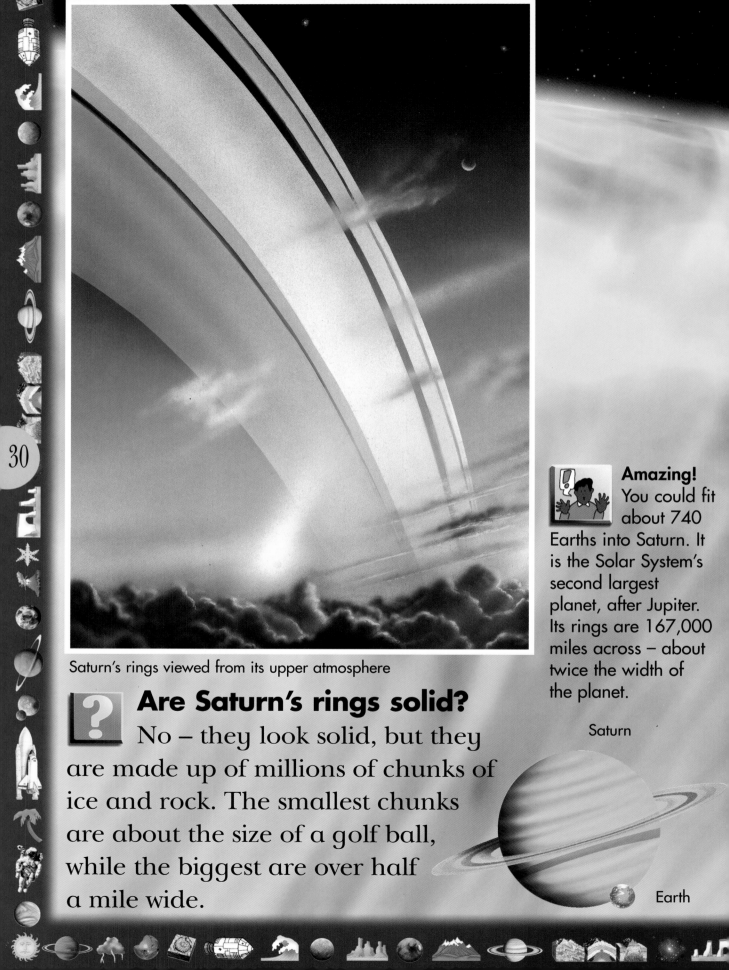

Saturn's rings viewed from its upper atmosphere

? Are Saturn's rings solid?

No – they look solid, but they are made up of millions of chunks of ice and rock. The smallest chunks are about the size of a golf ball, while the biggest are over half a mile wide.

Amazing! You could fit about 740 Earths into Saturn. It is the Solar System's second largest planet, after Jupiter. Its rings are 167,000 miles across – about twice the width of the planet.

Saturn

Earth

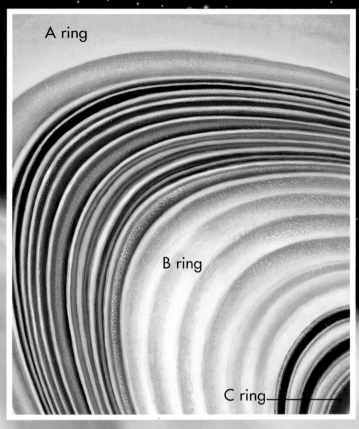

A ring

B ring

C ring

Saturn viewed
from above Titan

❓ How many moons does Saturn have?

Saturn has at least 18 moons, but there may be more. The biggest is Titan – the second largest moon in the Solar System. Titan is covered by clouds, so we can't see its surface.

❓ Do Saturn's rings have names?

Not really, but scientists have given each ring a letter so that they know which one they are talking about. There are seven main rings, of which the three brightest are A, B and C.

31

Is it true?
Saturn is light enough to float.

Yes. Saturn is made up of liquid and gas, with a small rocky center. It is so light that, if there was an ocean big enough, the planet would float on it like a boat!

William Herschel

? Which planet was found by accident?

Uranus was discovered in 1781. The man who found it, William Herschel, was not expecting to find a planet at all. He thought he was pointing his homemade telescope at a distant star.

? How many moons does Uranus have?

Uranus has at least 17 moons – but there could be more to discover. They are all named after characters from English literature. The main ones are Oberon, Titania, Umbriel, Ariel and Miranda. Ophelia and Cordelia are the closest.

Amazing! The poles on Uranus are warmer than the equator. Because Uranus is tilted on its side, the poles are the warmest places on the planet. Summer at the south pole lasts 42 years!

Approaching Uranus through its rings

Miranda

Uranus

Earth

Why is Uranus blue?

The bluish-green is the color of methane, a stinking gas that makes up part of Uranus's atmosphere. The other gases in the air there are hydrogen and helium – the gas we use to fill party balloons.

Is it true?
Uranus was nearly called George.

Yes. When Herschel discovered the new planet, he wanted to name it after the English king at the time, George III. In the end, it was called Uranus, after the Greek god of the sky.

George

? Which planet has pulling power?

Astronomers knew Neptune must be there before they saw it! They could tell something big was pulling Uranus and they were able to predict exactly where Neptune was – almost 2.8 billion miles away from the Sun.

Storm on Neptune

? What's the weather like on Neptune?

Very, very windy! Winds rip across the planet all the time, much faster than any winds on Earth. There are also lots of storms on Neptune, which show up as dark spots. This means Neptune's appearance is constantly changing.

Neptune seen from Triton

34

Is it true?
Triton is Neptune's only moon.

No. Neptune has seven other moons, but Triton and Nereid are the main ones. Triton is the biggest. It is 1,678 miles across – about four-fifths the size of our Moon.

? Where would you find pink snow?

When the gas nitrogen freezes, it looks like pink snow! There is frozen nitrogen at Neptune's north and south poles, and at the poles of its largest moon, Triton. So far from the Sun, Neptune and its moons are bitterly cold places.

Neptune's windy surface

Amazing! Triton is one of the coldest places ever recorded! The temperature on the ice-covered moon is minus 236° C. That's just 37°C away from being the lowest possible temperature in the entire Universe!

Pluto's icy surface is minus 220°C

? Which is the coldest planet?

Pluto is the coldest planet of all, which is not surprising, because it is usually the farthest from the Sun. Inside, it is made up of ice and rock, and the planet has a thick layer of ice over the top.

? Who found Pluto's moon?

An American called Jim Christy discovered Pluto's moon in 1978. He called it Charon, which was his wife's name, and also the name of the man who ferried people to the underworld in Ancient Greek mythology.

Is it true?
Pluto was named after a cartoon dog.

No. Pluto was the name of the Greek god of the underworld. Also, the first two letters of Pluto, "P" and "L" are the initials of Percival Lowell, who first predicted a planet beyond Neptune.

Amazing! Pluto is smaller than a country. Pluto is a tiny planet – the smallest in the Solar System. At 1,463 miles across, it is smaller than the United States or Russia!

❓ Is Pluto always farthest from the Sun?

Pluto is so far away from the Sun that it takes 248 years just to orbit it once! But Pluto's orbit is a funny shape. For 20 years of its orbit, Pluto dips in closer to the Sun than Neptune. When this happens, Neptune is the farthest planet in the Solar System.

USA

Pluto

Asteroids orbiting the Sun

? Are there any other planets?

There are lots of minor planets, known as asteroids, in our Solar System. About 3,500 of these lumps of space rock are orbiting the Sun.

Comet with its glowing tail

? Are there snowballs in space?

Yes – comets are balls of ice and rock. They go whizzing through the Solar System leaving behind a glowing tail of gas. As a comet gets closer to the Sun, it gets hotter and its tail becomes longer. Some comets even grow a second tail. In the past, the arrival of a comet was thought to be a magical event.

Shooting stars

Amazing! We can tell when comets will come back. Some comets follow a regular course, so we know exactly when we'll next see them. Halley's Comet will next fly past the Earth in 2061.

Is it true?
Asteroids weigh the same as the Earth.

No. Even if all of the asteroids in the Solar System were lumped together, the Earth would still weigh more than a thousand times as much.

? What is a shooting star?

A shooting star, or meteor, happens when a tiny space rock, called a meteoroid, enters Earth's atmosphere and burns up. We see it as a streak of light across the sky. Meteor showers happen when our planet passes through a group of meteoroids.

CHAPTER TWO

SPACE EXPLORATION

? Who made the first rockets?

The Chinese made the first "rockets" about 1,000 years ago, but they were more like fireworks than today's space rockets. They were flaming arrows that were fired from a basket using gunpowder.

Chinese "rocket"

Amazing! You don't need to be a rocket scientist to build rockets. Lots of people make mini rockets as a hobby. There is even a yearly contest, when people show off their latest creations!

Is it true?
Thrust SSC is a rocket-powered car.

No. Thrust SSC, the fastest car, has two jet engines. A jet engine could not power a space mission, because it needs air and there's no air in space.

Goddard's rocket

? When did the first liquid-fuel rocket fly?

In 1926, American Robert Goddard launched a 11 foot-long rocket. It flew about as high as a two-storey house, nowhere near outer space, and landed 184 feet away. The flight lasted just two-and-a-half seconds.

? Who built a rocket for war?

Wernher von Braun invented the V2, a rocket missile used by the Germans in World War II. After the war, von Braun moved to the United States, to help with the new American space programme.

von Braun and V2 missile

❓ Why do we need rockets?

Rockets are important for space travel. They are the only machines powerful enough to launch things into space, such as satellites, probes and people. All the parts needed to build space stations have been carried up by rockets.

Ariane releasing a satellite

 Amazing! The European Ariane rocket could carry a fully-grown elephant. Ariane's biggest payload (cargo) so far was a satellite which weighed 4.6 tons.

❓ How fast can a rocket go?

To escape from Earth's gravity, a rocket has to reach 25,000 mph – almost 20 times faster than supersonic Concorde. Once it is out in space, the rocket drops down to around 18,000 mph to stay in orbit.

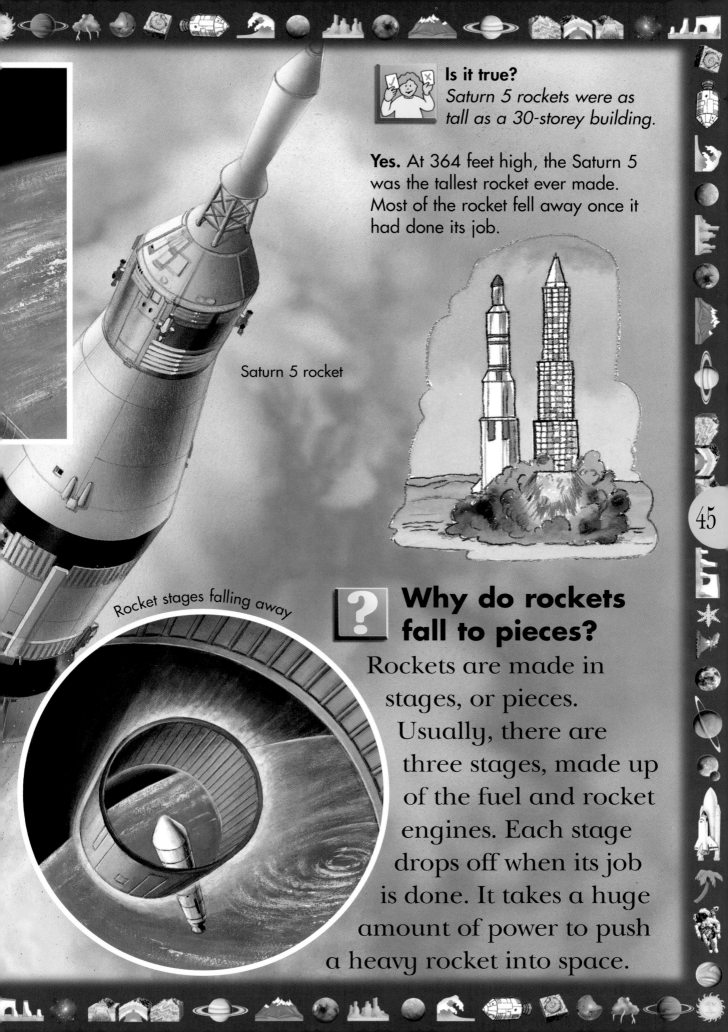

Is it true?
*Saturn 5 rockets were as
tall as a 30-storey building.*

Yes. At 364 feet high, the Saturn 5
was the tallest rocket ever made.
Most of the rocket fell away once it
had done its job.

Saturn 5 rocket

Rocket stages falling away

Why do rockets fall to pieces?

Rockets are made in
stages, or pieces.
Usually, there are
three stages, made up
of the fuel and rocket
engines. Each stage
drops off when its job
is done. It takes a huge
amount of power to push
a heavy rocket into space.

Amazing! The first living creature in space was a Russian dog, called Laika. She made a seven-day journey in the space capsule Sputnik 2 in November 1957.

Voskhod spacecraft

Yuri Gagarin and Vostok 1

? Who was the first man in space?

A young Russian pilot called Yuri Gagarin was the first person in space. He orbited the Earth in a small capsule called Vostok 1 on April 12th, 1961. His journey lasted less than two hours.

Valentina Tereshkova

Alexei Leonov making
the first spacewalk

? Who was the first woman in space?

The first woman in space was Russian, too. Valentina Tereshkova made a three-day space journey in Vostok 6 in 1963. The first American woman in space was Sally Ride, in 1983.

 Is it true?
A chimp could survive a space flight.

Yes. Ham was the first to try out the Mercury capsule in 1961. Despite travelling at 5,000 mph, the chimpanzee survived the 16-minute flight.

47

? Who took the first spacewalk?

The cosmonaut (Russian astronaut) Alexei Leonov took a ten-minute spacewalk on March 18th, 1965. To make sure he didn't float off, Leonov tied himself to his capsule.

Vostok capsule
returning to Earth

Which astronauts went to sea?

American astronauts returning to Earth landed in the sea and were picked up by helicopter. Their capsules had huge parachutes to slow down their fall, and rubber rings, so that they would float.

Amazing! Capsules got extremely hot. When a capsule re-entered Earth's atmosphere, its surface heated it up to 3,000°C – twice the temperature needed to melt iron. But they didn't melt, because they were protected by a special heat shield.

Apollo capsule splashing down

Who came down to Earth with a bang?

Russian capsules landed on hard ground. The cosmonauts bailed out and parachuted down the last few miles, but even so, many broke a few bones. They usually had to spend months in the hospital recovering from the landing!

Cosmonaut ejecting

Is it true?
Voskhod 2 got lost.

Yes. Voskhod 2 was the capsule carrying Alexei Leonov, the first spacewalker. The auto-pilot machinery went wrong, and the capsule ended up 620 miles off-course, in a snowy forest!

Mission Control

Who knew where astronauts landed?

Machinery on board a capsule was radio-linked to Mission Control (the people on the ground in charge of a space mission). This meant people knew exactly where to find the astronauts – usually!

Neil
Armstrong

? Who first set foot on the Moon?

The very first person to step on to the Moon was the American Neil Armstrong, in 1969. He had flown there in Apollo 11 with Buzz Aldrin, who followed him on to the Moon's surface, and Michael Collins.

 Amazing! There should have been seven manned missions to the Moon. Two days into Apollo 13's journey to the Moon, its oxygen tanks exploded. It took a nail-biting four days to bring its crew safely back to Earth.

50

Apollo 13

? How many Moon missions were there?

There were six manned Apollo landings on the Moon, and about 80 unmanned ones too. Apollo 17 landed the last astronauts on the Moon in 1972.

Is it true?
There are footsteps on the Moon.

Yes. There is no atmosphere on the Moon, which means there is no wind either. Tire tracks and footprints in the dusty surface will be there for hundreds of years.

? Who first drove on the Moon?

In 1971, Apollo 15 carried a Lunar Rover. David Scott and James Irwin drove the battery-powered buggy over the Moon's cratered surface, collecting samples of Moon rock.

Lunar Rover

51

52

Is it true?
There's only room for five astronauts aboard the shuttle.

No. The space shuttle was designed to carry eight astronauts, but it can carry ten in a pinch!

The shuttle is launched using two solid rocket boosters and three main rocket engines.

What was the first reusable spacecraft?

The space shuttle was the first spacecraft designed to be used more than once. Not every part is reusable, because it needs new rocket boosters for each flight. The shuttles have made over 100 missions into space. The first was Columbia, which blasted off in 1981. It orbited the Earth at about 17,250 mph – about ten times faster than a speeding bullet.

Rocket boosters fall away.

Liftoff

How many space shuttles are there?

There are four space shuttles in use today – Columbia, Discovery, Atlantis and Endeavour. The shuttle Challenger exploded shortly after liftoff in 1986. Shuttles are used for launching and repairing satellites, and space research.

Challenger explosion

 Amazing! The Russian space shuttle, called Buran, only flew once, in 1988. Buran was carried into space by a rocket. Unlike the American shuttle, it was unmanned.

How does the shuttle land?

At the end of its mission, the shuttle drops its speed to break orbit – on the opposite side of the world to the place it wants to land. Then it turns off its engines and glides like a bird, landing on a runway about an hour later.

Fuel tank falls away.

Shuttle re-enters atmosphere.

Shuttle glides back to runway.

Touchdown

Why do astronauts wear space suits?

Space suits act like a suit of armor. They stop an astronaut's blood boiling in space, and reflect the Sun's dangerous rays. They have a built-in backpack, containing an oxygen supply, battery and cooling system.

Cross-section of helmet shows communications headset.

Amazing! Astronauts are water-cooled! A system of tubes sewn into the space suit carries cool liquid around to keep the astronaut's temperature normal.

Cross-section of space suit shows water-cooling tubes stitched into undergarment.

Is it true? Cosmonauts took off in their underwear.

Yes. In the early days of Russian space travel, space suits were worn only for spacewalks. Some cosmonauts just wore their underwear at take-off time!

Cosmonaut in space capsule

? Do astronauts wear space suits all the time?

No. They wear them for spacewalks, and during take-off, landing or when they dock with another craft. The rest of the time, astronauts wear shorts and a T-shirt.

Backpack contains oxygen, batteries and water-cooling system.

Shuttle astronaut putting on space suit

? How do you go to the toilet in a space suit?

Astronauts often need to pee during take-off! Women wear an extra-absorbent diaper inside their suit. Some men prefer to do this too, but others wear a special sleeve that carries pee to a storage pouch inside the suit.

55

? **What's on the menu in space?**
Astronauts either add water to waterless food, or they eat ready meals, such as stew or pasta. Canned fruit, puddings, cookies, candy and gum are all on the menu, too.

Space shuttle galley

Is it true?
Astronauts eat freeze-dried ice cream.

No. The "astronaut ice cream" sold in stores isn't really eaten in space. But on the Mir space station, American astronauts took out an ice cream feast to share with the Russian cosmonauts!

Eating in space

? Why doesn't the food float away?

Everything floats about in space, so meals are eaten from trays stuck to astronauts' clothes. Drinks come in a cup with a lid and are sucked up through a straw.

Amazing! Some astronauts get space sickness! Floating makes many astronauts throw up, and if they're not careful the sick flies everywhere! Luckily, the sickness wears off after a day or two.

? How do astronauts wash?

The Skylab space station had a shower fitted with a vacuum cleaner to suck off the water, but there's no room for a shower on the shuttle. Astronauts use wet wipes, and clean their hair with rinseless shampoo.

Skylab shower

Amazing! There were spiders in space. Arabella and Anita had a special mission on Skylab. Scientists wanted to see if space affected how spiders spin webs.

Soyuz spacecraft docked with Salyut 1 space station

? Which was the first space station?

The first manned space station was Salyut 1, launched in 1971, which had room for three crew. It was meant to go into permanent orbit around the Earth, but its orbit was a bit too low.

? What happens in a space station?

Astronauts live in space stations for weeks or even months. They do experiments and find out more about space. They also do lots of exercise, to stay fit and healthy.

Exercise in space

Is it true?
Your bones get weaker in space.

Yes. This isn't serious on short missions, but no one knows what would happen if you spent years in space.

? What's the biggest space station?

The International Space Station (ISS) will be the biggest ever space station when it's finished in 2003. The first module was launched in 1998 and the space station's parts are being built by 16 countries.

International Space Station

? Who needs a tool kit in space?

Astronauts need tools to build the ISS and repair satellites. In 1993, a space shuttle crew repaired the Hubble Space Telescope.

Working in space

MMU in action

? What's an MMU?

MMU stands for Manned Maneuvring Unit. It's like an armchair that carries an astronaut around in space, when he or she is outside the spacecraft. It uses 24 little gas jets to move backward or forward, up or down.

Is it true?
The space shuttle has an arm.

Yes. It has a robot arm with a hand that can grip at the end. It can be controlled by astronauts inside or outside the shuttle. The robot arm is useful for picking up objects in space.

Amazing! Astronauts train underwater. Working underwater gives astronauts an idea of how it will feel to float in space. Water makes an astronaut's body move in the opposite direction when they try to pull or push something, just as it would in space.

Astronaut using headset radio

61

How do astronauts talk to each other?

Space is an airless vacuum that won't carry sound. Even if they were yelling, astronauts outside their craft wouldn't be able to hear each other, so they stay in touch by radio.

? Has anyone ever been to Mars?

No, not yet, anyway! The distance from Earth to Mars varies from 35 million miles to 250 million miles. Even at its closest, Mars would be a six-month journey away.

Sun

Earth's orbit

Mars's orbit

Pathfinder landing

Is it true?
Vikings landed on Mars.

Yes. In 1976, two space probes called Vikings 1 and 2 landed there. During their mission, they collected samples and took over 3,000 photos.

? What used balloons to land on Mars?

The Mars Pathfinder probe entered the Martian atmosphere on July 4th, 1997. It used a parachute and rockets to slow down and then a bundle of balloons inflated around it so that it could bounce safely down on to the surface.

Amazing! Pathfinder landed in a river! Although there is no liquid water on Mars now, the rocky plain where Pathfinder touched down showed signs that water had flowed there once.

Pathfinder

Which robot explored Mars?

Pathfinder carried a robot car called Sojourner, which was radio-controlled from Earth. It had a camera and devices for studying the soil and rock.

What was the first satellite in space?

Sputnik 1 was the first satellite to orbit the Earth. It was launched by the Russians in October 1957 and took 90 minutes to circle the planet.

Sputnik 1

Is it true?
A person could have fitted in Sputnik 1.

No. The satellite was less than 2 feet across – smaller than most beach balls! Sputnik was just a radio transmitter really, but it was very important for space exploration.

Can you see any satellites from Earth?

Yes. You can see satellites moving across the sky when the Sun is shining on them but it is dark on Earth. The best times to spot satellites are the two hours after sunset and the two hours before sunrise.

Amazing! Satellites are powered by the Sun. Rocket power takes satellites up into orbit, but once they're there, they use special solar panels to collect energy from the Sun. This is turned into electricity to power the satellites' batteries.

Solar Maximum satellite

? Why don't satellites fall down?

Earth's gravity tries to pull a satellite down, but the satellite's speed as it orbits the Earth tries to fling it into space. Usually, the two forces cancel each other out – but there have been mistakes!

Halley's Comet

The Giotto space probe visited Halley's Comet in 1986 and took brilliant photos of the comet's rocky core. Even though Giotto kept a safe distance of about 400 miles, its special protective shields got covered in icy dust.

66

Giotto

Amazing! A probe carries a message for aliens. The Pioneer 10 probe was fitted with a plaque, just in case it's ever found by aliens. It shows a man and woman, and a map to show where Earth is in the Universe.

Pioneer 10's plaque

Is it true?
A probe was made out of junk.

Yes. Magellan, sent to visit Venus in 1989, was made up of spare parts from other missions.

? Which spacecraft flew furthest?

Voyager 2, launched in 1977, has flown past Jupiter, Saturn, Uranus and Neptune. Now it is beyond our Solar System, heading into interstellar space.

Voyager 2 passing Jupiter

Cassini

? Which probe is as big as a bus?

The bus-sized Cassini space probe has another probe, called Huygens, on board. It should reach Saturn in 2004. Cassini will beam data back to Earth about Saturn's rings, moons and the planet itself.

Is it true?
We could never breathe on Mars.

No. We couldn't breathe in the atmosphere there as it is, but we could build airtight cities and grow plants there that would make oxygen for us.

? **Might there be pirates in space?**

If we ever set up space mining stations, spacecraft would zoom about the Solar System with very valuable cargos. Space pirates might try to board cargo-carrying craft to rob them!

Will we ever live on the Moon?

There might be a Moon Base, one day. The Moon is only three days away and its low gravity makes it easy to land spacecraft there. It would be a good place for telescopes, because there is no atmosphere to distort the pictures.

Moon Base of the future

 Amazing! People are planning a space hotel. Vacations in space are not far off. There are plans for a doughnut-shaped space hotel, using old shuttle fuel tanks as rooms!

Will we ever live on other planets?

It will take a lot more probe missions before we could consider building bases on other planets. But if travel to other stars ever became possible, the outer planets could act as useful "gas stations."

Space tanker near Saturn

CHAPTER THREE

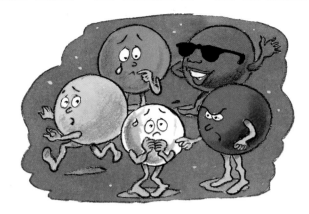

BEYOND OUR SOLAR SYSTEM

What is the Universe?

Every person, planet, star and galaxy is part of the Universe – and even every empty space! The Universe is the biggest thing we have a word for.

Amazing! The Universe is too big to measure in miles. Even if you could travel at the speed of light, it would take at least 15 billion years to cross it – as far as we know!

What's outside the Universe?

It's impossible to say. Scientists are still trying to guess, by using clues left behind from the birth of our Universe. They are pretty sure there would be no time, distance or things there.

Where are we in the Universe?

People once thought Earth was at the center of the Universe. Now we know Earth is one of many planets moving through space. It's hard to tell where we are because we can't see the Universe's edges.

Voyager space probe looking at our galaxy in the distant future

Our Solar System

Local stars

Our galaxy

Local group of galaxies

Local super group of galaxies

The Universe

Is it true?
There are more stars than people.

Yes. As a rough guess, scientists think that there are about 1.8 million million stars for every human being alive in the world today.

When did the Universe begin?

Scientists have argued about this for centuries. At the moment, most people agree that the Universe began between 12 and 15 billion years ago. It all started with a mind-boggling explosion called the Big Bang.

Amazing! The Big Bang was super-hot! Scientists don't even bother writing out all the zeros in its temperature. They write $10^{27}°C$, meaning 10 with 27 zeros after it!

What was the Big Bang?

It was a huge explosion, that created all the mass and energy in our Universe in less than a second! The effects of the blast are so strong that the Universe is still expanding.

? What if the Big Bang happened again?

It couldn't happen again in our Universe, but some people think it may be happening millions of times, making millions of different universes. Only a few would last as long as ours – most would pop like soap bubbles.

There might be millions of universes.

Is it true?
You could see the Big Bang through a telescope.

Nearly. Our telescopes aren't powerful enough yet – but we can already see light from the other side of the Universe that began its journey just after the Big Bang!

The Universe expands from the Big Bang.

? Will the Universe ever end?

Some cosmologists (people who study the Universe) believe that the Universe will eventually stop expanding outward. They think it will shrink back to nothing in an event called the Big Crunch!

Is it true?
The Universe might just fizzle out.

Yes. If the Universe keeps spreading out forever, it will get quite boring. After the stars have burnt out, there'll just be lumps of rock and dust floating around doing nothing!

The Universe shrinks back to the Big Crunch.

❓ Why would it crunch?

The Universe is still blowing up, but there are lots of heavy things in it. Just like a toy balloon, which has run out of puff, gravity might pull the Universe back to where, and how, it started.

Amazing! The Universe might go on forever! Some cosmologists think that the Universe will never stop expanding. They don't think gravity will ever be able to stop it, so it will just get bigger and bigger.

❓ Will I see the Big Crunch?

Not unless you live forever! Even if the Universe does stop expanding, it will take about another 15 billion years to collapse in on itself in a Big Crunch.

What are star nurseries?

New stars are born in star nurseries – huge clouds of gas and dust known as nebulae (or nebula if you're just talking about one). Nebulae are some of the most beautiful sights that powerful telescopes have ever revealed.

Stars are born in gaseous clouds called nebulae.

 Amazing! A star can be born in a horse's head! The Horsehead Nebula is a glowing cloud of gas in another galaxy. It has a lump shaped like a horse's head, where stars are being born.

How are stars born?

The gases in a nebula gradually gather together into spinning balls. They spin more and more quickly, until they get amazingly hot and a big blast, called a nuclear reaction, begins. When this happens, a baby star begins to glow.

What are stars made of?

Stars are mostly made of two gases, hydrogen and helium. Helium is the gas used to fill party balloons. There are lots of layers inside a star, with gases moving around in each one.

Surface of star

The convection zone transfers hot gases to the surface of the star.

The conduction zone carries energy from the core outward.

Core of star

Is it true?
You are made of stardust.

Yes. Everything in space, including you, is made out of elements, such as carbon and silicon. All of these were cooked up in stars, which formed from the first matter in the Universe.

Which stars live together?

Our star, the Sun, is all alone, but some stars, called binary stars, are in pairs. They seem to spin around each other. Very close pairs do one turn of this "dance" in just hours!

80

Our Sun is a medium-sized star.

How long do stars shine for?

It depends. Very hot, bright stars burn up all their energy in a few million years. A star like our Sun, which is only medium-hot, can shine for billions of years.

? What is a white giant?

White giants are really huge, hot stars that appear to be white. They can be 20 times bigger than our Sun. Rigel is a white giant shining about 60,000 times more brightly than our Sun.

Our Sun compared to a white giant

Amazing! Small stars are called dwarfs! Astronomers know that stars come in lots of different sizes. To make it easier to describe the sizes, they call big stars giants and little ones dwarfs.

Is it true?
Most stars are yellow.

No. Stars hotter than our Sun often shine a bright pale blue, while other stars can sometimes appear red or white. Only a few are yellow.

81

? Which stars go out with a bang?

Really massive stars, at least eight times bigger than our Sun, die in an explosion called a supernova. For a few days supernovas shine so strongly that, here on Earth, we can see them during the day.

Amazing! Supernovas are a very rare sight. Only a few supernovas have been seen in our galaxy in the last 1,000 years. One visible to the naked eye was seen in 1987, in a nearby galaxy called the Large Magellanic Cloud.

82

? What is a white dwarf?

A white dwarf is a dying star. Its gas has burnt off, and a planet-sized, white-hot and incredibly dense core

A white dwarf shedding the gases of its old self

is all that is left. Over billions of years, this fades and dies. Sirius B, or the "Pup," is a white dwarf.

? What is a red giant?

A red giant is an old star that has swollen up. Depending how big it gets, it might blow up or fade out. Astronomers think that our Sun will grow into a red giant in about five billion years' time. Betelgeuse is a red giant, and is 500 times bigger than our Sun.

Our Sun compared to an enormous red giant

A red giant swallows up a planet.

83

Is it true?
Dead stars are called black dwarfs.

Yes. Once a white dwarf has cooled and stopped shining, it becomes a dead, black dwarf.

What is the Little Green Man?

LGM stands for "Little Green Man." LGM1 is a light deep in space that flashes 30 times a second. It is a pulsar – a tiny, dense neutron star (the remains of a supernova) that flashes out light and radio signals as it spins.

A pulsar flashing out light and radio signals, near a red giant

Is it true?
Scientists thought pulsar signals were messages from aliens.

Yes. The astronomers in Cambridge, England, who discovered LGM1 wondered at first if they'd come across an alien distress beacon or some other kind of coded message!

Amazing!
Neutron stars are super-heavy! They can be just 12 miles across, but weigh 50 times more than planet Earth!

Radio telescopes

❓ How many pulsars are there?

No one is sure, but hundreds have been found since the 1960s, when scientists first spotted the Little Green Man. Special telescopes called radio telescopes are used to "listen" for more pulsars.

❓ Do all pulsars spin at the same speed?

No – even the slowest spin about once every four seconds, but the fastest whizz round many hundreds of times in a single second! Their incredible speeds are thought to be caused by magnetic forces left by a supernova.

What is a black hole?

A black hole is a place in space that forms when a really huge star collapses. Everything around a black hole is sucked into it, like water down a plug hole. The force of gravity in a black hole is so strong that nothing can escape from it – not even light.

Black hole

Amazing! No one has ever seen a black hole. Because beams of light cannot escape black holes, astronomers cannot see them – even with the most powerful telescopes.

What is dark matter?

Dark matter is what scientists call all the stuff in the Universe that they know is there but can't find! They think it might be made of ghostly little particles called neutrinos.

Neutrinos

Is it true?
Black holes turn you into spaghetti.

Yes. Scientists think that, in the last moments before you disappeared forever into a black hole, the force of gravity would stretch you until it pulled you apart. They call this being "spaghettified!"

87

Dark matter

How do we know that dark matter is there?

Scientists can guess how much matter is in the Universe by measuring how galaxies move. This shows them that stars and planets only make up a small part of the Universe. The rest is invisible!

What is a galaxy?

A galaxy is a group of stars, dust and gases that are held together by gravity. Our galaxy is the Milky Way and contains about 100 billion stars, one of which is our Sun.

Is it true?
All galaxies have names.

No. Each one that we detect is given numbers and letters, but only some, such as our Milky Way, are given a name as well. "Galaxy" comes from the Ancient Greek word for "milk."

How many galaxies are there?

No one knows for sure. There might be hundreds of billions of galaxies – and new ones are forming right now at the edges of the Universe.

On a clear night you can see the Milky Way.

88

Spiral, oval and irregular galaxies

? Are there different kinds of galaxies?

Yes – each galaxy is unlike any other. Some are bright and some are dim. There are three basic galaxy shapes, though – spiral, elliptical (oval) and irregular. Of course, irregular just means no particular shape!

Amazing! There's a galaxy named after a wide-brimmed Mexican hat. "Sombrero" is the nickname of galaxy M104. Can you guess the galaxy's shape?

Galaxies can form in many weird and wonderful shapes.

❓ What shape is our galaxy?

Our galaxy, the Milky Way, is a spiral galaxy. Viewed from above, it looks like a giant Danish pastry with swirls of white icing. From the side, it looks more like two fried eggs stuck back-to-back!

Amazing! Our galaxy has a twin. Andromeda is the biggest galaxy near the Milky Way. It's the same age and a similar shape, but has many more stars.

❓ What's at the middle of the Milky Way?

The center (the two "egg yolks") is called the nuclear bulge. There's probably a monster black hole there, more than a million times bigger than our Sun. Scientists call the black hole Sagittarius A*.

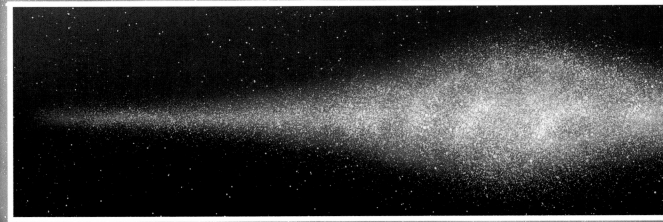

A side view of the Milky Way seen from deep space

How big is the Milky Way?

The Milky Way is almost too big to imagine. It would take the world's fastest jet, the Blackbird, about 30 billion years to cross the galaxy.

Blackbird

Is it true?
We're near the center of the Milky Way.

No. Our Solar System is closer to the edge, on one of the spiraling arms. Our Sun takes 225 million years to go around the center once!

Do galaxies stick together?

Some galaxies are all alone in space, but others huddle together in clusters. Together with 30 other galaxies, our Milky Way and its twin, Andromeda, are part of the Local Group cluster.

Amazing! The Local Supercluster contains several thousand galaxies, and is more than 100 million light-years across. A light year is about 5,866 billion miles.

Cluster of galaxies

The background shows two galaxies colliding.

Are some galaxies cannibals?

Some scientists think that Andromeda gobbled up other galaxies. It has a double center, which might be the remains of another galaxy. One day, Andromeda may eat up the Milky Way. It gets 180 miles closer to us every second!

? What is a supercluster?

It's a cluster of clouds of clusters! The Local Group that contains our Milky Way is part of a cloud called the Canes Venatici cloud. Together with about six other clouds of galaxies, it is part of the Local Supercluster.

Supercluster of galaxies

93

Is it true?
We're part of the biggest galaxy cloud in the Local Supercluster.

No. The biggest is the Virgo I cloud, which contains a fifth of all the galaxies in the supercluster. It's pulling the other clouds in the cluster towards it.

The Moon's gravity pulls a meteorite crashing into its surface.

? What is gravity?
Gravity is one of the basic forces in the Universe, like electromagnetism. It makes things with mass pull toward each other. More massive objects, such as the Earth, pull smaller objects, such as you, toward them until they stick together.

Isaac Newton

Is it true?
An apple taught us about gravity.

Maybe. According to legend, super-scientist Isaac Newton first realized how gravity works over 330 years ago, after gravity pulled an apple from a tree he was sitting under, and it landed on his head!

? Is the Universe expanding evenly?

No – the force of gravity stops everything from flying outward. Lumpy bits of space become even lumpier, moving at different speeds. Gravity locks together little pockets of space and matter, such as galaxies.

Galaxies locked together by the force of gravity

Amazing! There are walls in space! Galaxies aren't evenly spaced through the Universe. They are arranged more like walls around emptier regions of space. One wall has already been measured – it's about a billion light years across!

? What is the Great Attractor?

It's a strange little knot in space that has the pulling power of 50 million billion Suns, but is not a black hole.

? Is time the same everywhere?

No, time slows down when you're traveling very quickly. Brainy boffin Albert Einstein predicted this odd effect in 1905 but we only proved it a few years ago by sending a super-precise atomic clock into orbit around the Earth.

Albert Einstein

Is it true?
Einstein was the world's best mathematician.

No. Although he was very clever, Albert Einstein often asked his wife to check over the trickier math for him.

? Could time stand still?

Only if you traveled as fast as the speed of light – which most scientists agree is impossible! Some scientists think that time must stand still inside a black hole, but who'd want to find out?

Black hole

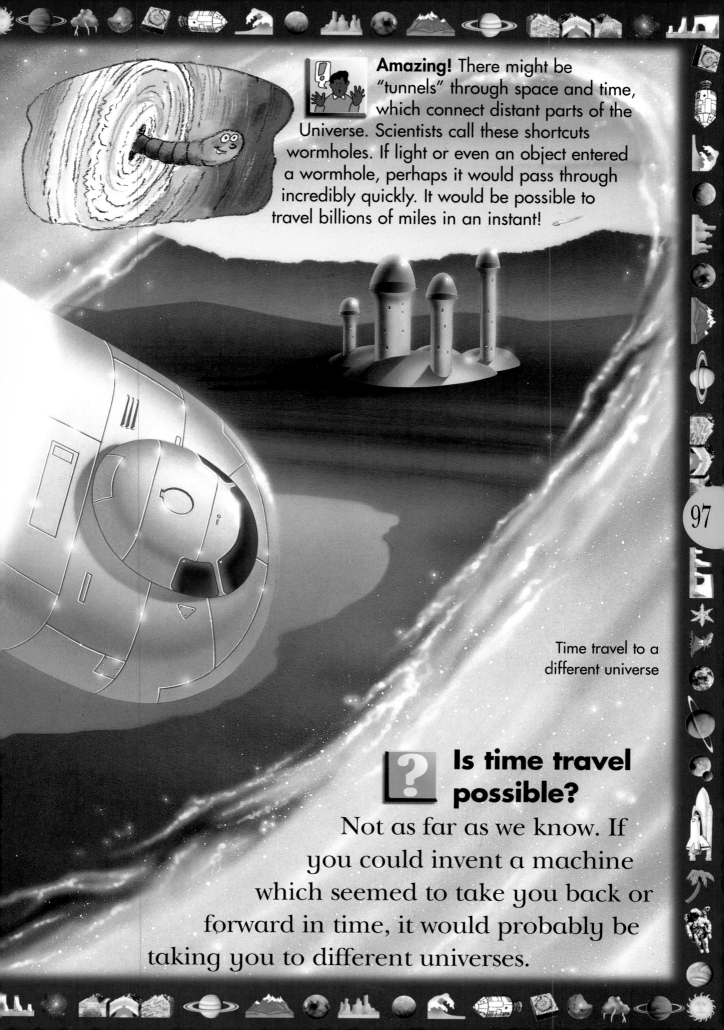

Amazing! There might be "tunnels" through space and time, which connect distant parts of the Universe. Scientists call these shortcuts wormholes. If light or even an object entered a wormhole, perhaps it would pass through incredibly quickly. It would be possible to travel billions of miles in an instant!

Time travel to a different universe

? Is time travel possible?

Not as far as we know. If you could invent a machine which seemed to take you back or forward in time, it would probably be taking you to different universes.

❓ Is there anybody out there?

We don't know. Life might be such a fluke that it only exists on Earth. But if scientists can find just one other place where there is life, we'll know life's no accident – and that there could be millions of aliens!

❓ How will we find out?

People around the world have joined the Search for Extra-Terrestrial Intelligence (SETI). They spend their spare time on computers, studying waves from space, hoping to find alien messages.

Radio astronomy center

? Do aliens know about us?

It's unlikely. Humans have only been making radio waves for about a century, so aliens would have to live very nearby to tune in.

Amazing! Some people think that the Universe is a living thing – and that the planets, stars and galaxies are just parts of its "body!"

Aliens with the Pioneer space probe

Is it true?
Aliens have visited the Earth.

Probably not. There's no proof that aliens have visited us. Even if they could travel at the speed of light, they would take at least four years to reach us from the nearest stars.

CHAPTER FOUR

LOOKING AT THE NIGHT SKY

? Who gazes at the stars?

We all enjoy looking up at the starry night sky, especially on a clear moonless night, away from bright city lights. Some people even star-gaze as a job. They are scientists called astronomers. Astronomy is the science of studying space and all the objects in it.

Astronomer and telescope

Amazing! You can see about 2,500 stars in the night sky! When the sky is clear, you can see that many different stars even without a telescope!

? Can anyone be an astronomer?

Anyone can learn about stars as a hobby, but it takes years of study to do it as a job. You'll need books of star charts and maps, so you can recognize what you see. Binoculars or a telescope will let you see further.

Studying a star chart

Is it true?
You can see the Moon's craters through binoculars.

Yes. Binoculars allow you to see the Moon's surface so clearly that you can make out individual craters – from 248,000 miles away!

? Can you only see the Moon and stars at night?

The Moon and stars are easiest to spot, but even without a telescope you will see meteors (shooting stars) and the brighter planets, such as Venus, Jupiter or Mars. Venus shines white and is nicknamed the "evening star." Jupiter looks greeny-blue and Mars glows red.

Meteor shower

103

Who built a tomb for the Sun god?

The Ancient Egyptians thought their kings were the Sun god, Re, who had come down to Earth. They buried kings in huge tombs called pyramids, maybe because the pyramid shape pointed at the sky.

Pyramid

Who built a stone circle for the Sun?

No one knows exactly why Stonehenge, a huge stone circle in southwest England, was built by Druids over 4,000 years ago. Its doorway would have framed the sunrise on the longest day of each year.

Is it true?
Stonehenge was a primitive computer.

No. But in the 1960s an American scientist called Gerald Hawkins said it was. He thought Stonehenge was built to work out when eclipses would happen.

104

Ancient Druid ceremony at Stonehenge

Who thought the sky was a goddess?

The Egyptians thought the night sky was the arched body of a goddess, called Nut. Today we know Nut's body matches the view of the Milky Way from Ancient Egypt.

The Milky Way seen above the pyramids

Ancient Egyptian wall painting showing the goddess Nut

Amazing! The pyramids have secret Sun passages! Tunnels were built so the buried king could see the sunset on a particular day each spring.

105

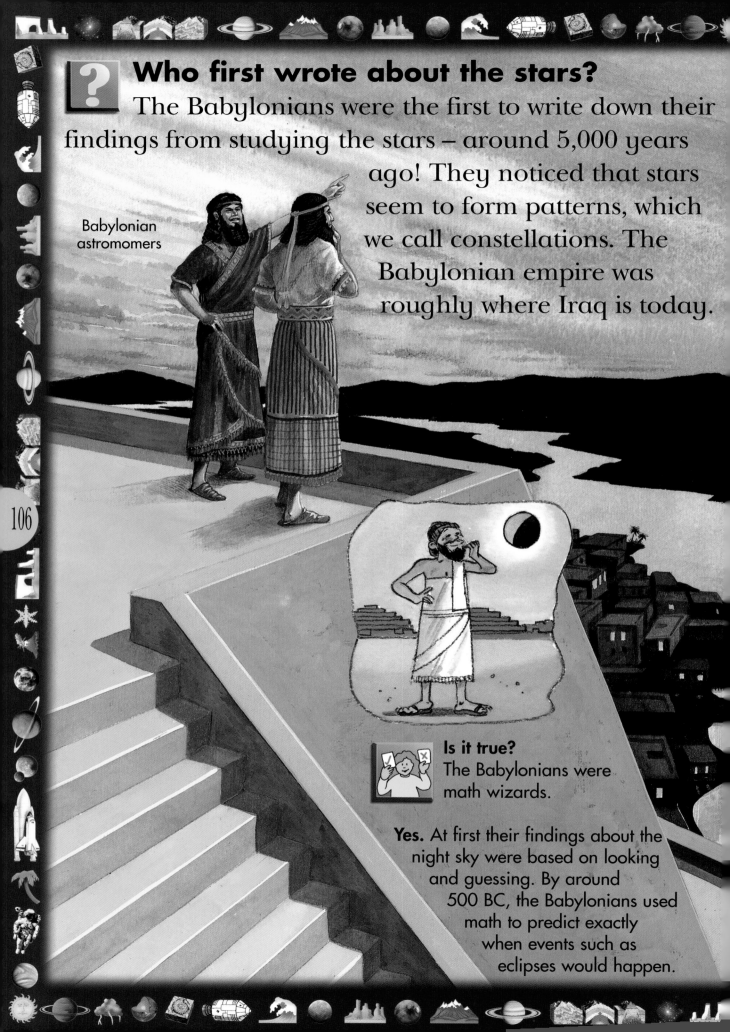

❓ Who first wrote about the stars?

The Babylonians were the first to write down their findings from studying the stars – around 5,000 years ago! They noticed that stars seem to form patterns, which we call constellations. The Babylonian empire was roughly where Iraq is today.

Babylonian astromomers

Is it true?
The Babylonians were math wizards.

Yes. At first their findings about the night sky were based on looking and guessing. By around 500 BC, the Babylonians used math to predict exactly when events such as eclipses would happen.

How do we know about the first astronomers?

The Babylonians didn't write on paper like we do. They wrote on clay tablets, so fragments have survived. Scientists called archaeologists dig in the ground for clues about ancient peoples such as the Babylonians.

Babylonian writing on a clay tablet

Amazing! The Babylonians didn't see the same night sky as us. There were no twinkling satellites, and the stars were in different places because our Solar System has moved since then.

What was a Babylonian year like?

The Babylonians worked out a 12-month year. Each month began with the first sight of the crescent Moon. The months were called Nisannu, Ayaru, Simanu, Du'uzu, Abu, Ululu, Tashritu, Arahsamnu, Kislimu, Tebetu, Shabatu and Addaru.

Clay tablet

Amazing! An eclipse changed the course of history. Soldiers from Athens in Ancient Greece lost a battle after being spooked by an eclipse of the Moon. Their rivals, the Spartans, were the winners.

? Who thought the Sun was as wide as a ruler?

The Greek thinker Heraclitus thought the Sun was just 12 inches across and a new one was made each morning. So even though the Ancient Greeks were smart, they didn't get everything right!

Heraclitus

Who named groups of stars?

In AD 150, the Greek astronomer Ptolemy wrote a book about the stars, describing 48 different constellations (star groups). He named the groups after characters from Greek myths, such as Perseus, the hero who rescued the princess Andromeda. We still use Ptolemy's names today.

Perseus and Andromeda

Is it true?
People once thought the Earth was flat.

Yes. Even up to the 1500s most people believed this. They thought that if you sailed too far, you could fall off the edge!

Aristotle

Who worked out the Earth is round?

The Ancient Greek thinker Aristotle realized that the Earth must be round in the 330s BC. He worked this out when he was watching a lunar eclipse, because he saw that the Earth made a circular shadow on the surface of the Moon.

Why do stars make patterns?

Constellations are the patterns that bright stars seem to make in the night sky, such as a cross, a letter "W" or the shape of a person. The stars look close together – but that's just how we see them from Earth. Really they are scattered through space and nowhere near each other.

 Amazing! The night sky is divided into 88 different star patterns. Nearly 50 were first described 2,000 years ago!

What we see

Actual position of stars

Earth

What is the zodiac?

For astronomers, the zodiac includes the 12 constellations that the Sun passes through during a year. We can't see the Sun doing this, though. The Sun's light is so bright that we cannot see the constellations during the day.

Aquarius

Sagittarius

Virgo

Libra

Capricornus

Scorpius

Zodiac constellations

Which stars make a hunter?

Orion is a constellation named after the legendary Greek hunter. Lots of stars make up the shape. Rigel is the brightest and makes one of the hunter's legs. The next-brightest is Betelgeuse, which shines a reddish color.

Orion

Leo

Gemini

Aries

Cancer

Pisces

Taurus

111

Is it true?
Astrologers are specialist astronomers.

No. The zodiac signs that astrologers use for horoscopes have the same names as the zodiac bands in astronomy. They don't match with the astronomical constellations, though.

❓ How did sailors know where they were going?

Out at sea, there are no landmarks. In the Middle Ages, sailors had special instruments that used the position of the Sun and stars to tell them where they were. These included compasses, astrolabes and cross-staffs.

Sailor and cross-staff

Amazing! The first astrolabes were made 1,500 years ago! Indian and Arab astronomers used pocket-sized instruments called astrolabes in the AD 500s.

Is it true?
Astrolabes only worked at night.

No. You could use the position of the Sun instead of the stars, when you were sailing during the day. You looked at its position compared to the horizon.

What is the pole star?

The only star which doesn't appear to move is above the North Pole. Sailors could tell where they were by looking at the pole star – it's lowest in the sky at the Equator.

Path of the stars with the pole star in the middle

How did an astrolabe work?

An astrolabe had two disks, one with a star map, and the other with measuring lines and a pointer. You compared them with the Sun or a star and the horizon to work out your position.

Astrolabe

Who made the first telescope?

Hans Lippershey, a Dutch man who made spectacles, probably made the first telescope in 1608. He noticed that if he put two lenses at different ends of a tube and looked through them, objects seemed to be nearer and clearer.

Is it true?
Newton saw a rainbow in his telescope.

Yes. Isaac Newton noticed that the edges of objects seemed colored when you looked through a telescope. That's how he began to work out that clear white light is made up of many different colors.

114

Hans Lippershey with his telescope

Simple cross-section of a telescope

? How does a telescope work?

The lens (curved piece of glass) at the front end of a telescope gathers light to make an image of an object that is far away. The lens at the back magnifies the image so it can be seen more clearly.

? Who put mirrors in a telescope?

Isaac Newton was the first person to make a mirror or reflecting telescope. He replaced the front lens with a dish-shaped mirror at the back. The mirror reflected the image on to a smaller mirror, and then into the eye.

Newton's reflecting telescope

115

Amazing! You can see Saturn's rings through a telescope. Telescopes magnify images (make them bigger) so much that you can even make out Saturn's faint rings – which are about 800 million miles away!

Who said that planets go around the Sun?

Nicolaus Copernicus explained this idea in a book in 1543. The problem was, the Church stated that God had put the Earth at the center of the Universe. You could be put to death for saying that the Earth went around the Sun.

Nicolaus Copernicus

Who was put on trial for star-gazing?

Few scientists were brave enough to say that they agreed with Copernicus's findings that the Earth went around the Sun. The Italian astronomer Galileo was – and was put on trial for his ideas in 1634.

Is it true?
The Church accepted that Galileo was right in the end.

Yes. The Church eventually agreed that the Earth and other planets traveled around the Sun. But they didn't do this until 1992 – 350 years after Galileo's death!

Galileo on trial

❓ Who first used a telescope for astronomy?

Galileo started making telescopes in 1609, not long after Lippershey made his. Galileo was the first person to realize how useful a telescope would be for looking at the night sky. Because he could see more clearly, he made lots of important new finds, such as discovering four of Jupiter's moons.

Amazing! Copernicus explained the seasons. By showing that the Earth goes around the Sun and also spins at the same time, Copernicus explained why some times of the year are warmer than others.

Galileo looking at the night sky

? Where do astronomers put their telescopes?

Observatories are buildings where astronomers go to look at the sky. They house the most powerful telescopes on Earth. The telescopes are usually kept in a room with a dome-shaped roof. Observatories have other instruments too, such as very precise clocks, to help keep accurate time and records.

Pulkovo Observatory, Russia

118

Mount Cerro Observatory, Chile

? Where's the best place to build an observatory?

Where you'll get the clearest view! Most are built away from city lights. Mountain-tops are best of all, because they poke above any clouds that might spoil the view.

No. The Kitt Peak National Observatory in Arizona, USA has the most optical telescopes. One of them, the Mayall Telescope, is 13 feet across!

 Amazing! The Ancient Babylonians used observatories. They did their star-gazing from stepped towers called ziggurats.

? How can a telescope see through the roof?

Telescope in a domed observatory

It doesn't have to – an observatory's domed roof is specially designed to slide open at night, so that the picture through the telescope isn't distorted (blurred) by looking through a window. The telescope can be pointed at any place in the sky.

119

How deep is space?

Early astronomers thought that all the stars were the same distance from us, forming a simple shell around the Earth. Now we know that some stars are relatively close to us, and others are trillions of miles away.

Gaseous clouds in deep space

Amazing! Galaxies move so quickly they are different colors. The light waves from them change, just as a fire truck's siren sounds lower after it zooms past. We use the color to measure the galaxies' speed.

Are there candles in space?

Not really. But we can see how far away a galaxy is by the brightness of a special type of star, called a "standard candle." The further away the galaxy, the dimmer the candle.

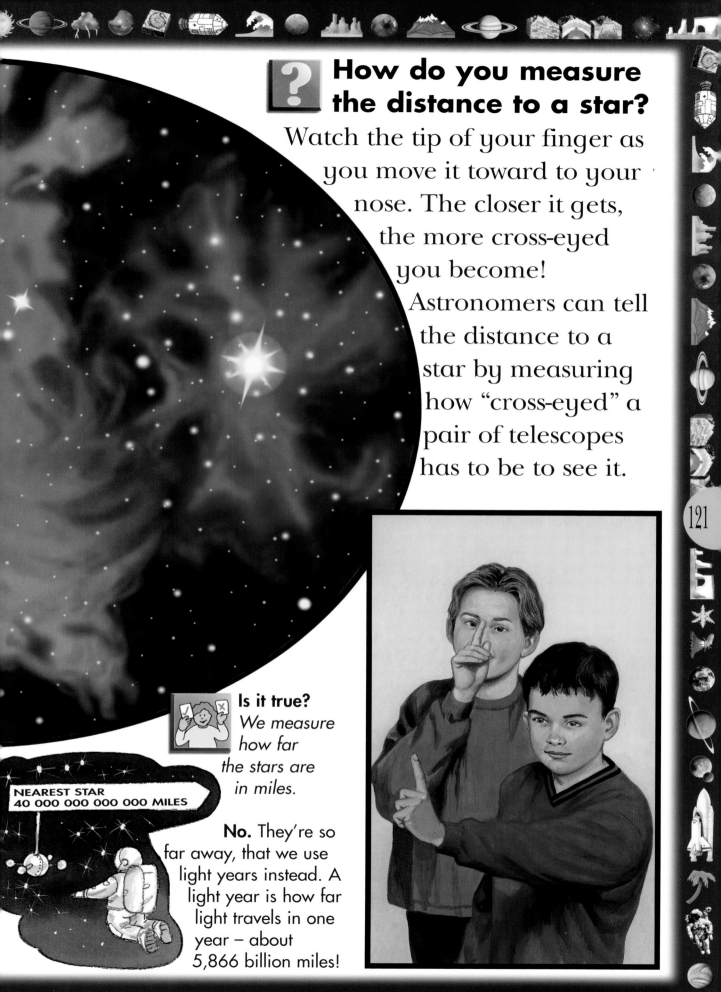

How do you measure the distance to a star?

Watch the tip of your finger as you move it toward to your nose. The closer it gets, the more cross-eyed you become! Astronomers can tell the distance to a star by measuring how "cross-eyed" a pair of telescopes has to be to see it.

121

NEAREST STAR 40 000 000 000 000 MILES

Is it true?
We measure how far the stars are in miles.

No. They're so far away, that we use light years instead. A light year is how far light travels in one year – about 5,866 billion miles!

Who made the first radio telescope?

Radio telescopes are like giant satellite dishes that pick up invisible radio waves and similar waves, instead of light rays. Unlike light, radio waves can travel through cloud, so radio telescopes can be built just about anywhere! An American called Grote Reber made the first one in the 1930s.

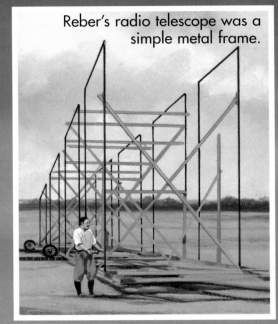

Reber's radio telescope was a simple metal frame.

Amazing! A telescope can be 5,000 miles long. The Very Long Baseline Array (VLBA) stretches across the USA. It has ten different dishes and produces the best-quality radio images of space from Earth yet!

Which are the most powerful radio telescopes?

The ones that are made up of several different radio dishes, such as the Very Large Array (VLA) in New Mexico, USA. The VLA has 27 dishes, each 82 feet across. Scientists compare the findings from all 27 dishes to get super-accurate results.

VLA, Socorro, New Mexico

Where is the biggest radio telescope?

The world's biggest single-dish radio telescope was built in Puerto Rico in the Caribbean about 40 years ago. It is 985 feet across – so it would take you more than ten minutes to walk around the edge of it.

Radio telescope, Puerto Rico

Is it true?
Only ten astronomers are allowed to use the VLA.

No. It is used by over 500 astronomers a year. Some study our near-neighbors in the Solar System, while others peer way beyond our galaxy to others in deepest space.

What's a gravity telescope?

A gravity telescope uses laser beams to measure its own length. As a gravity wave passes through Earth from space, it stretches the telescope by less than the width of an atom! Four huge gravity telescopes were built at the end of the 1990s.

Gravity telescope

Amazing! The biggest gravity wave telescope is over 2 miles long! No one knows yet what new things gravity wave telescopes will help astronomers discover.

Can we see black holes?

We can through a gravity telescope. Although light can't escape a black hole, gravity can. When a black hole swallows up a star, for example, there's a "ripple" of gravity through space. Gravity wave telescopes spot the ripples.

Black hole

? What's the weirdest telescope?

The Super Kamiokande telescope near Tokyo is just a big tank full of very pure water, buried deep underground. Very sensitive cameras detect teeny-weeny particles called neutrinos zooming through the Earth, by recording microscopic flashes of light in the water.

Neutrino detector

Is it true?
Neutrinos have a dark secret.

Yes. Scientists think the Universe is full of something heavy, which they call dark matter. Neutrinos may be part of it!

Are there telescopes in space?

Yes – the first one went up in the 1960s. Space is a perfect place for looking at the stars. The sky is always dark and cloudless. Away from Earth's pollution and wobbly atmosphere, the stars shine steadily and brightly, instead of twinkling as they do to us on Earth.

X-ray multi-mirror telescope

Are there observatories in space?

Yes – some observatories use powerful gamma rays, which can penetrate all the gas and dust in the galaxy, to show us what is happening at its center. The Compton gamma ray observatory was launched into space by the shuttle.

Gamma ray observatory

Which telescope is in orbit?

The most famous is the Hubble Space Telescope, which was carried into orbit on the space shuttle Discovery in 1990. It circles the Earth every 90 minutes, about 375 miles above us. It beams radio signals of information to astronomers on Earth.

Hubble Space Telescope

Is it true?
Telescopes can look back in time.

Yes. Because of the time it takes X-rays to travel through space, Chandra can see quasars as they were ten billion years ago!

Amazing! Hubble runs on Sun-power. Hubble's two "paddles" are solar panels. They gather energy from the Sun and change it into electrical energy. The energy is used to focus the telescope and beam data home.

127

What's better than a powerful telescope?

Seeing for yourself in close-up – but it's too dangerous and expensive to send astronomers deep into space. That's why space probes are such important tools. Space probes are fitted with cameras. They beam back close-up photos of faraway planets and comets.

Cassini-Huygens spacecraft

Amazing! Chandra is a billion times more powerful than the first X-ray telescope. If telescopes keep improving at this rate, we'll be able to see the farthest edges of the Universe in 30 years' time!

Is it true?
A probe found a watery world.

Yes. The Voyager 2 probe photographed what might be water on Jupiter's moon, Europa. If there is life out there, probes will probably find it first.

? Could we build Very Large Arrays in space?

Scientists are already testing a cluster of satellites that fly in perfect formation, using laser beams. The same technology will be used to create a string of small satellite telescopes, making one huge "eye" in space.

VLA in space

129

? Could we build an observatory on the Moon?

The dark side of the Moon would be a perfect site. Always pointing away from the Earth, it is shielded from man-made X-rays. But building there would be very expensive.

Moon observatory of the future

CHAPTER FIVE

PREHISTORIC LIFE ON EARTH

? How old is the Earth?

Earth is millions and millions of years old. In fact, our planet is four-thousand-six-hundred-million years old. When the Earth's age (4.6 billion years) is written as a number, it looks like this: 4,600,000,000. It's hard for us to imagine anything so old.

Earth today

 Amazing! Some of Earth's oldest known rocks are found in Scotland. They are about 3.5 billion years old.

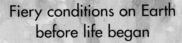
Fiery conditions on Earth before life began

? Has there always been life on the Earth?

Nothing at all lived on the Earth for the first billion (1,000 million) years of the planet's existence. The conditions were not right for life. There were no plants or animals of any kind. Earth was a dangerous place where life could not survive.

132

200 million years ago

150 million years ago

80 million years ago

? Has the Earth always looked the same?

These maps show how Earth's land and sea looked in the past. To fit everything on them, Earth has been drawn as an oval. For a long time, all land was joined together in one giant mass. Over millions of years it broke up into smaller pieces. They turned into today's continents.

Is it true?
The continents are still moving.

Yes. The continents move about one and a half inches each year – the length of your little finger. Millions of years in the future, Earth will look very different from today.

❓ When and where did life on Earth begin?

Life on Earth began about 3.5 billion years ago. The first life appeared in the sea. It was born into a world that looked very different from today. The atmosphere was filled with poisonous gases. The sky was pink, and the sea was rusty-red.

Conditions on Earth were hostile when life first began.

Is it true?
Earth is the only planet with life on it.

Maybe. This is one of the greatest unsolved mysteries. Life probably does exist on other planets besides Earth, but nothing has been found so far. The search continues.

134

? How did life begin?

It is thought that life began when lightning hit the sea. Lightning sent energy into the water. Chemicals in the sea were mixed together by energy. New substances, called amino acids, were made, from which life was able to grow.

Amazing! The first living things on Earth were so small you could fit thousands of them on the head of a pin.

? What were the first living things?

The first living things were bacteria. They lived in the sea. Some bacteria changed into algae, which were simple plants. Algae lived in the sea in masses, like huge blankets. They made oxygen, which helped to turn the sky and sea blue.

Closeup of bacteria

What animals lived in the sea?

For millions of years all life lived in the sea. It was home to a huge variety of creatures, such as shellfish, worms, sponges and jellyfish. None of these animals had backbones.

Early sea life

Is it true?
The very first fish didn't have jaws.

Yes. Instead of jaws to open and close their mouths the very first fish sucked food into their mouths. They are called jawless fish.

Cladoselache (an early shark)

Acanthodians

Which animals first had backbones?

About 510 million years ago, new kinds of animals appeared in the sea. They were the first fish, and they were the first animals with backbones. Because they had backbones to support their bodies they could become much larger.

Heliobatis fossil

Amazing! In the Indian Ocean is a fish called a *coelacanth*. It has hardly changed for 350 million years. It is a living fossil.

Dunkleosteus

Cheirolepis

Placoderms

Sacabambaspis

What were early fish like?

Giant sharks, much larger than any alive today, swam through the oceans. They hunted smaller fish. Armored fish grew bony plates to protect their soft bodies. Other fish had bodies covered in sharp spines.

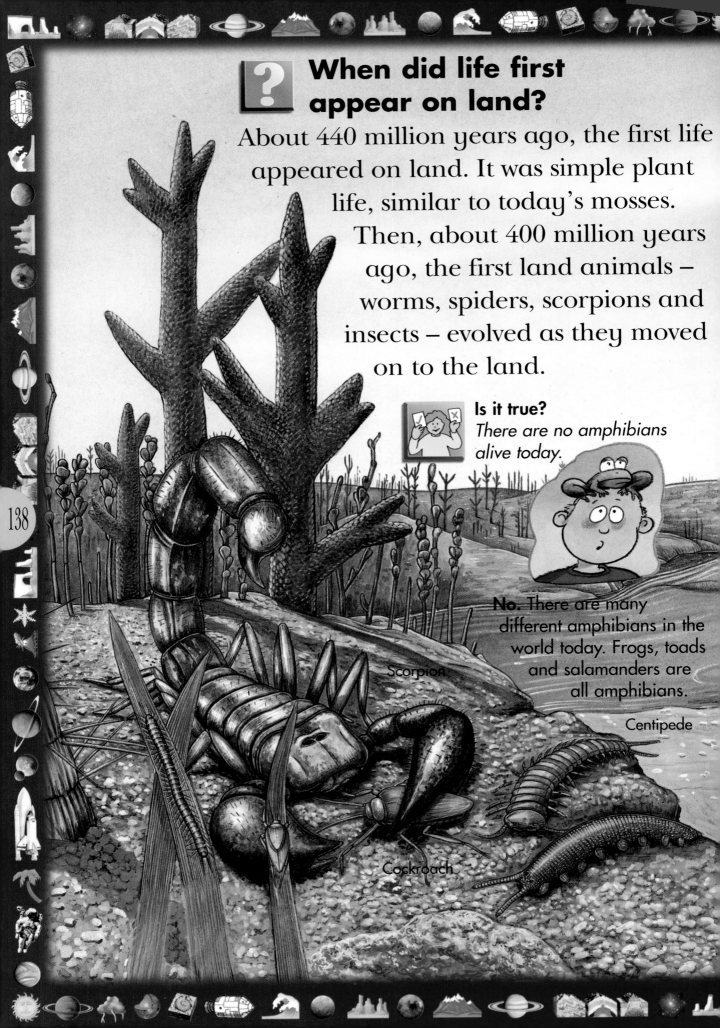

❓ When did life first appear on land?

About 440 million years ago, the first life appeared on land. It was simple plant life, similar to today's mosses. Then, about 400 million years ago, the first land animals – worms, spiders, scorpions and insects – evolved as they moved on to the land.

Is it true?
There are no amphibians alive today.

No. There are many different amphibians in the world today. Frogs, toads and salamanders are all amphibians.

Scorpion

Centipede

Cockroach

138

Why did some fish grow legs?

Some fish began to live in shallow water. It was difficult to swim in the shallows. To help these fish move around they grew short legs. Some of them also grew lungs, which meant they could breathe air. These animals could live in water and on land.

Acanthostega (an early amphibian)

Amazing! The lungfish is one of today's fish that can live out of water. It can breathe air.

139

Which animal lives in water and on land?

An animal that can live in water and on land is called an amphibian. It means "double life." The first amphibians appeared by 350 million years ago. Gradually, they spent more and more time on land.

Ichthyostega (an early amphibian)

? **What are reptiles?**

About 300 million years ago, some amphibians changed into reptiles. They could live on land all the time. Reptiles have backbones and scaly skin, and most lay eggs. Many reptiles, such as crocodiles, spend lots of time in the water, but they can't breathe underwater. They use the Sun to keep their bodies warm.

Is it true?
Some early reptiles had sails, on their backs.

Yes. *Dimetrodon* had a skin "sail" on its back. It soaked up the Sun's heat, and controlled the animal's body temperature.

Hylonomus

❓ What did reptiles eat?

The first reptiles, such as *Hylonomus*, were small lizard-like animals that ate tiny creatures. Reptiles learned how to run quickly so they could catch fast-moving insects. As reptiles became larger, they caught and ate bigger prey, including other reptiles. Some reptiles only ate plants.

Amazing! A small animal found in Scotland, in rocks that are 350 million years old, might be one of the first reptiles. But some scientists say it was an amphibian.

Hylonomus and dragonfly

141

❓ Which reptiles had fur?

Some prehistoric reptiles grew fur on their bodies to keep themselves warm. These were the cynodonts. They lived about 245 million years ago. Over time they changed into a completely new group of animals, called mammals.

Cynognathus (a cynodont)

Thrinaxodon (a cynodont)

Crocodilian

Compsognathus

What were dinosaurs?

Dinosaurs were members of the reptile family. They first appeared about 225 million years ago. For 160 million years dinosaurs ruled the Earth. They walked on straight legs, tucked underneath their bodies, and they lived on land. The word dinosaur means "terrible lizard."

Hadrosaur
(a plant-eater)

Is it true?
All dinosaurs were big.

142

No. The tiny *Compsognathus* was about the same size as a chicken.

Deinonychus
(a meat-eater)

What did dinosaurs eat?

Some dinosaurs were carnivores. This means they ate meat and fish. Some were herbivores. These dinosaurs ate plants. A third group were omnivores. They had a mixed diet and ate both meat and plants. Some dinosaurs swallowed stones, which crushed food inside their stomachs so it was easier to digest.

Seismosaurus
(a plant-eater)

Amazing! When *Ankylosaurus* filled its bony plates with blood it could have blushed pink!

What color were dinosaurs?

No one knows what color dinosaurs were. Perhaps some had skins that matched their surroundings, making them hard to see. Some might have had bright markings to attract mates, or scare others away.

Tyrannosaurus rex and Hypsilophodons

? Could dinosaurs make noises?

Dinosaurs had voice boxes, which means they could make noises. *Parasaurolophus* had a long, hollow bone on top of its head. Perhaps it forced air through the bone to make a deep, hooting sound.

Parasaurolophus

Amazing! A dinosaur has gone into space! In January 1998, a fossil *Coelophysis* skull traveled on board the space shuttle Endeavour. The 220-million-year-old fossil flew four million miles around the Earth.

Maiasaura adult and young

? Did dinosaurs care for their young?

Yes, some did. *Maiasaura*, whose name means "good mother lizard," cared for its young. Parents looked after them until they were old enough to take care of themselves.

Is it true?
Every animal on Earth died out with the dinosaurs.

No. Lots of animals survived. Birds, mammals, amphibians, insects, small reptiles (lizards), fish, spiders, snails and crocodiles all lived.

? Why did dinosaurs die out?

Dinosaurs died out 65 million years ago. Many people think this was because a big meteorite (a space rock) hit the Earth. It sent dust into the air which blotted out the Sun. Dinosaurs died because they were too cold and hungry.

Meteorite hitting Earth

Which creatures flew in the sky?

At the same time as dinosaurs walked on the land, other reptiles flew in the sky and swam in the sea. The sky reptiles were pterosaurs, which means "winged lizards." Their wings were not made from feathers, like a bird's, but from stretched skin.

Quetzalcoatlus

Liopleurodon

Which creatures swam in the sea?

The sea was home to many different reptiles. Some had very long necks. These were plesiosaurs, which means "near lizards." Others looked like today's dolphins. They were ichthyosaurs, which means "fish lizards." Ichthyosaurs were fast and agile swimmers.

Ichthyosaur

Pteranodon

Rhamphorhynchus

147

Is it true?
One pterosaur was as big as a small plane.

Yes. *Quetzalcoatlus* was an enormous pterosaur. It had wings 40 feet across. It is the biggest flying creature ever.

Plesiosaur

Feeding pterosaur

Amazing! The short-necked plesiosaur *Liopleurodon* grew to 75 feet and weighed 50 tons. It was a giant sea monster!

❓ What did pterosaurs eat?

Some pterosaurs ate fish, which they scooped from the sea with their long beaks. Some pterosaurs may have held lots of fish inside their cheek pouches, as pelicans do today.

? What are birds?

Birds are animals with backbones, they lay eggs, can make their own body heat, and have wings. They are also the only animals with feathers. Not all birds can fly. The first birds lived at the same time as the dinosaurs.

Prophaeton

Phororhacos

Is it true?
Ostrich eggs are the biggest eggs ever laid by a bird.

No. The extinct bird *Aepyornis* laid the biggest eggs of all time. Each one was about the size of 150 hen's eggs.

Hyracotherium
(a very small, early kind of horse)

? Where do birds come from?

Birds evolved from small, meat-eating dinosaurs. Fossils show that some of these dinosaurs had feathers. They are called "dinobirds." The first "dinobirds" probably could not fly.

Caudipteryx

Fossilized Archaeopteryx

Archaeopteryx

Amazing! Today's hoatzin bird, which lives in South America, has claws on its wings when young – just like *Archaeopteryx*, its prehistoric ancestor did.

149

? Which was the first true bird?

The first true bird – a bird that could fly – appeared about 150 million years ago. It is known as *Archaeopteryx*, which means "ancient wing." It had claws on its wings.

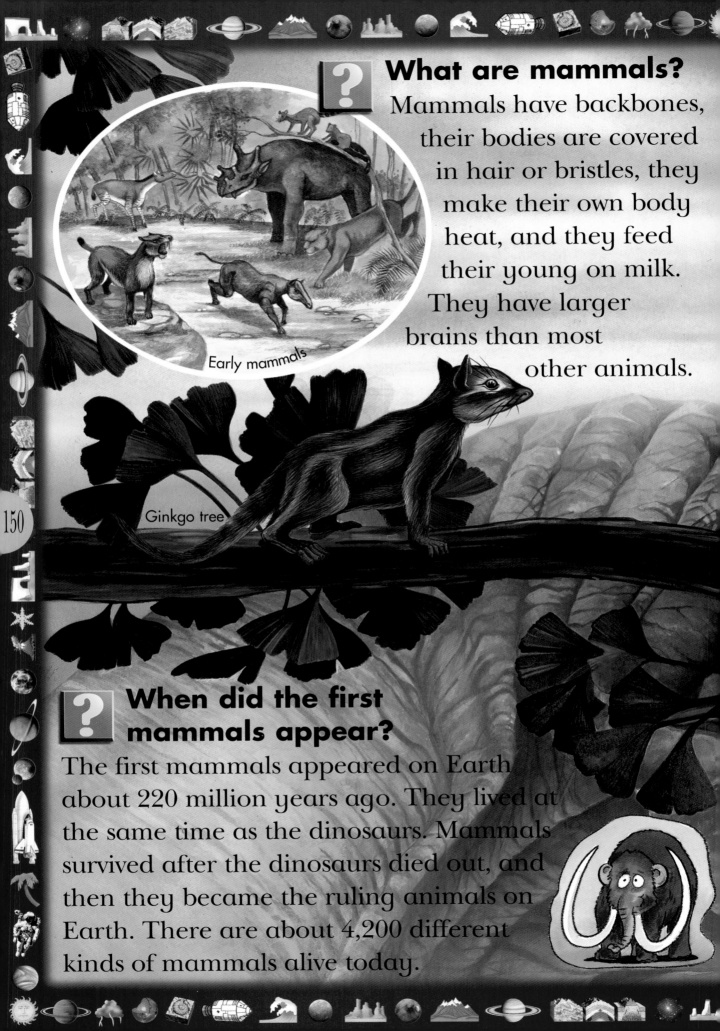

What are mammals?

Mammals have backbones, their bodies are covered in hair or bristles, they make their own body heat, and they feed their young on milk. They have larger brains than most other animals.

Early mammals

Ginkgo tree

When did the first mammals appear?

The first mammals appeared on Earth about 220 million years ago. They lived at the same time as the dinosaurs. Mammals survived after the dinosaurs died out, and then they became the ruling animals on Earth. There are about 4,200 different kinds of mammals alive today.

Did mammals only live on land?

Mammals came to live in all of Earth's habitats. Many lived on land, but some, such as bats, were able to glide through the air on wings of skin. Other mammals swam in the sea, such as whales, dolphins and seals.

Basilosaurus

Tyrannosaurus rex

Megazostrodon

Is it true?
The elephant is the largest land mammal ever to have lived.

No. *Indricotherium* was the largest land mammal. It was almost 26 feet tall and as heavy as four elephants.

151

Amazing!
Woolly mammoths were big elephants with extra-long tusks up to 10 feet long. Their bodies were covered in fur.

Amazing! One *Australopithecus* is called Lucy. Her bones were found in 1974, when a song with the name Lucy in it was on the radio. She was named after it.

A group of human ancestors collecting fruit

Australopithecus skull

❓ Who were our ancestors?

Our earliest ancestors were apes that walked upright on two legs. *Australopithecus*, meaning "southern ape," was one of the first apes to walk upright. It lived at least three million years ago, and was short and hairy.

Yes. Compared with a modern human, an adult *Australopithecus* like Lucy was very short – only about 4 feet tall.

How did they live?

Australopithecus probably lived in small family groups. These bands of human ancestors wandered across the grassy plains of their homeland. They ate fruit, leaves, seeds and roots. They may have used sticks to help dig for food, and might have eaten meat, too.

153

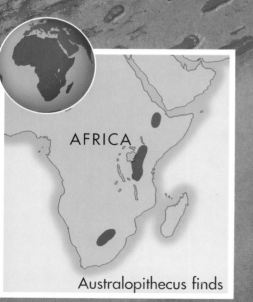

AFRICA

Australopithecus finds

Where did they live?

Australopithecus lived in Africa. Bones of this upright ape have been found in several countries, including Tanzania, Ethiopia and South Africa. Africa is where human species probably began, a few million years ago.

Homo
habilis

Homo
erectus

? Who were the very first humans?

The first people we think of as humans appeared in Africa. About two million years ago, *Homo habilis* (handy man) appeared. Then, more than one million years ago, *Homo erectus* (upright man) appeared, but they weren't modern humans.

Hand ax

Fire-making tool

Flint knife

? Did they have any tools?

Homo habilis was the first tool-user. This is why he is called "handy man." He made simple tools, such as choppers, from pebbles. The tools made by *Homo erectus* were better. He shaped stones into hand axes, and he was the first to use fire.

What did they eat?

Homo habilis and *Homo erectus* ate meat and plants. Meat probably came from dead animals that they found. They may have hunted for some small animals. Plants gave them berries and leaves. They used stone tools to cut and scrape their food.

Is it true?
Homo erectus was a wanderer.

Yes. More than one million years ago, *Homo erectus* began to move out of Africa, traveling to Europe and Asia.

Homo erectus people hunted and gathered their food.

Amazing! *Homo erectus* had fire. Fire provided warmth, gave heat for cooking, and offered protection from predators.

155

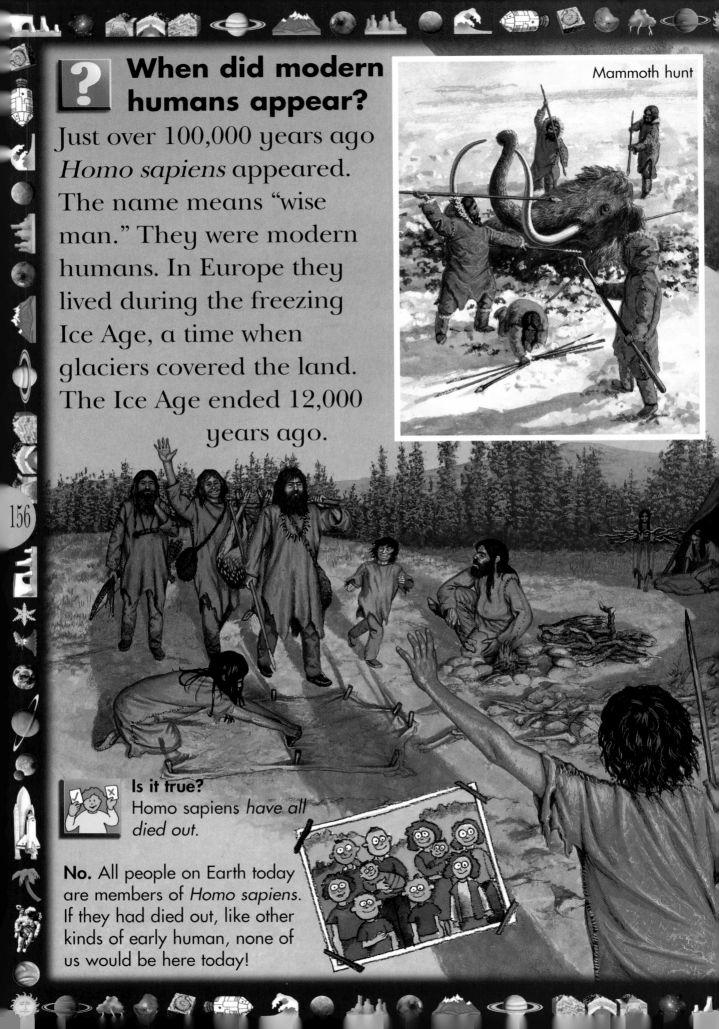

? When did modern humans appear?

Just over 100,000 years ago *Homo sapiens* appeared. The name means "wise man." They were modern humans. In Europe they lived during the freezing Ice Age, a time when glaciers covered the land. The Ice Age ended 12,000 years ago.

Mammoth hunt

Is it true?
Homo sapiens *have all died out.*

No. All people on Earth today are members of *Homo sapiens*. If they had died out, like other kinds of early human, none of us would be here today!

? Where did they live?

Homo sapiens first appeared in Africa, and from there, they spread out across the world. They lived in cave entrances, and in places sheltered by overhanging rocks. In the open they made huts from branches, covered with skins.

As the climate grew warmer, Homo sapiens people migrated across the world.

Amazing! People who lived during the Ice Age played musical instruments. They made whistles from bones, and drums from shoulder-blades.

Animal carving

Cave painting

? Were they artists?

The humans who lived in Europe during the Ice Age were among the first artists. They painted pictures of horses, bison and deer on the walls of their caves. Bone and ivory were carved into figures of animals and people.

How do we know about life in the past?

We find out about life in the past by looking for evidence. Fossils are one kind of evidence. They are the remains of living things that have been preserved. Objects made by humans, such as stone tools, are another kind of evidence.

A collection of fossils

Is it true?
Plants can't be fossilized.

No. Plants can become fossils, in the same way that animals can. By studying them we learn about the plants that once grew on Earth.

158

1

2

3

4

How is a fossil made?

It takes millions of years to make a fossil. The pictures on the left show how it happens. (1) An animal dies. Its body sinks to the bottom of a lake. (2) Sand and silt cover its body. (3) The flesh rots away. Minerals seep into the bones and turn them to stone. The animal is now a fossil. (4) The fossil is found.

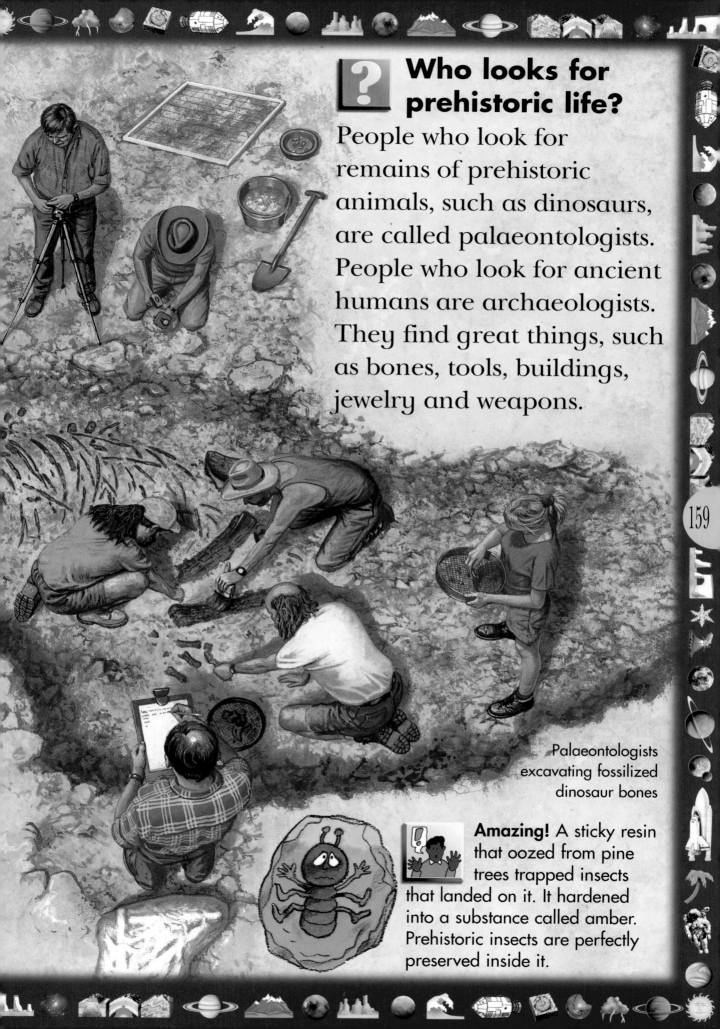

? Who looks for prehistoric life?

People who look for remains of prehistoric animals, such as dinosaurs, are called palaeontologists. People who look for ancient humans are archaeologists. They find great things, such as bones, tools, buildings, jewelry and weapons.

Palaeontologists excavating fossilized dinosaur bones

Amazing! A sticky resin that oozed from pine trees trapped insects that landed on it. It hardened into a substance called amber. Prehistoric insects are perfectly preserved inside it.

CHAPTER SIX

EXPLORING EARTH

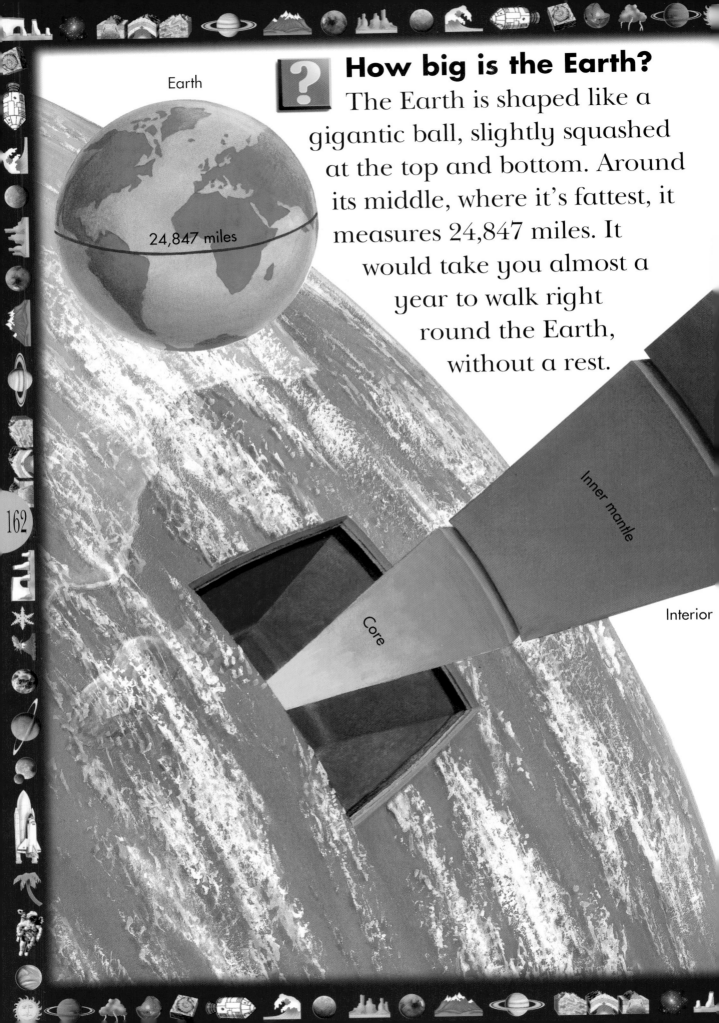

Earth

24,847 miles

How big is the Earth?
The Earth is shaped like a gigantic ball, slightly squashed at the top and bottom. Around its middle, where it's fattest, it measures 24,847 miles. It would take you almost a year to walk right round the Earth, without a rest.

Inner mantle

Core

Interior

162

What's inside the Earth?

The Earth is made up of layers of rock and metal. We live on the hard, rocky surface, called the crust. Below, the layers are so hot that they've melted and turned runny. The center of the Earth is a ball of almost solid metal.

Crust and atmosphere

Lithosphere

Outer mantle

Amazing! People used to think the Earth was flat. If they sailed too far in one direction, they thought they'd fall off the edge!

What are the continents?

The Earth's rocky crust is cracked into several gigantic pieces and lots of smaller chunks. The large pieces contain the seven continents - Africa, Antarctica, Asia, Australasia, Europe, North America and South America. Which of the continents do you live on?

Earth's main continental plates

163

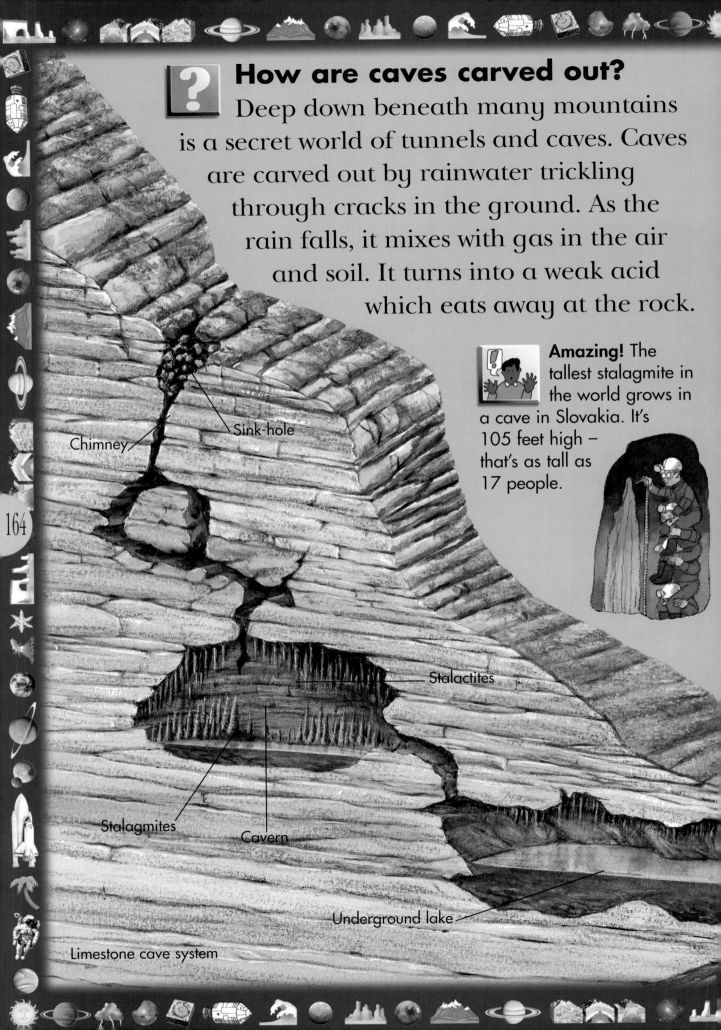

? How are caves carved out?

Deep down beneath many mountains is a secret world of tunnels and caves. Caves are carved out by rainwater trickling through cracks in the ground. As the rain falls, it mixes with gas in the air and soil. It turns into a weak acid which eats away at the rock.

Amazing! The tallest stalagmite in the world grows in a cave in Slovakia. It's 105 feet high – that's as tall as 17 people.

Chimney

Sink-hole

Stalactites

Stalagmites

Cavern

Underground lake

Limestone cave system

Mammoth Caves, Kentucky

? Where are the longest caves?

The Mammoth Caves in Kentucky are the longest caves on Earth. They stretch for 347 miles. The biggest single cave is the Sarawak Chamber in Malaysia. Its floor is the size of 30 football fields.

? Which caves are art galleries?

Thousands of years ago, prehistoric people sheltered in caves, and painted pictures on the walls. The best art gallery is in the Lascaux Caves in France. The walls are covered with hundreds of animals, including bison and mammoths.

Prehistoric cave art

Is it true?
Potholers are people who explore caves.

Yes. Even though it's wet, cold and dark underground. The deepest a potholer has ever been is 4,947 feet in a cave in Russia.

How are mountains built?

Some mountains are built when two pieces of the Earth's crust bump or crash into each other. The rock in between is pushed up into giant fold mountains. Other mountains are made when huge blocks of rocks are squeezed up.

Himalayas

Mountains are formed as rocks are squeezed upward by the force of India pushing against Asia.

Over millions of years, the island of India moved toward the continent of Asia, until eventually they met.

Amazing! The first people to climb to the top of Mt Everest were Sherpa Tenzing Norgay and Edmund Hillary in 1953.

Himalayan mountain range

Why are mountains shrinking?

It takes millions of years for mountains to grow. But many are shrinking every day. Mountains are being worn away by wind, frost and ice. They attack the peaks and break off chips of rock.

Shrinking mountain

Where are the highest mountains?

The highest mountains in the world are the Himalayas in Asia. This massive mountain range has twelve of the world's 14 highest peaks, including Mt Everest. At 29,029 feet, it's the highest mountain on Earth.

Is it true?
The higher up a mountain you go, the hotter it gets.

No. The higher you go, the colder it gets. That's why the tops of some peaks are capped in snow – and why many mountain animals have warm, winter coats.

167

Where are the Poles?

The North and South Poles are at either end of the Earth. The North Pole is surrounded by the frozen Arctic Ocean. The South Pole is in the middle of icy Antarctica.

North Pole

South Pole

Amazing! The coldest place on Earth is Vostok in Antarctica. Here temperatures can plummet to a f-f-freezing minus 89°C.

Why are the Poles cold?

The Poles are the coldest places on Earth. They're battered by blizzards and covered in ice and snow. The Poles are cold because the Sun's rays hit them at a slant, so they're spread out and very weak.

Sun's rays

Pole

Equator

? Who reached the South Pole first?

The first person to reach the South Pole was Norwegian explorer Roald Amundsen in December 1911. He beat the British team of Captain Scott by about a month. Exhausted and suffering from frostbite, Scott died on the way home.

Is it true?
Penguins live at the North Pole.

No. Penguins only live around the South Pole. But you might bump into a polar bear at the North Pole.

Captain Scott in the Antarctic

170

Amazing! In 1912, the luxury liner, Titanic, hit an iceberg and sank in the North Atlantic. It was on its maiden (first) voyage from Southampton, England to New York.

Iceberg seen from underwater

Belgium

United Kingdom

Belgium

France

What are icebergs?

Icebergs are giant chunks of ice that break off the ends of glaciers and drift out to sea. Only about a tenth of an iceberg shows above water. The rest is hidden under the sea. This makes them very dangerous to passing ships and boats.

Which was the biggest iceberg?

The biggest iceberg ever was seen near Antarctica. It was about the size of Belgium! The tallest iceberg was more than half as high as the Eiffel Tower in Paris.

Is it true?
*Baby icebergs
are called calves.*

Yes. When a baby iceberg
breaks off a glacier, it is
called "calving." Even
smaller icebergs are called
"bergy bits."

? Which is the longest glacier?

Glaciers are enormous
rivers of ice that flow
slowly down a
mountainside.
The Lambert-Fisher Glacier in
Antarctica is over 370 miles long.
It's the longest glacier in the
world. About a tenth of the Earth is
covered in icy glaciers.

Glacier

? Why does the sea flow in and out?

Twice a day, the sea washes on to the shore at high tide. Then it flows back out again at low tide. The tides are caused by the Moon and Sun pulling the sea into giant bulges on either side of the Earth.

 Amazing! If all the coasts were straightened out, they'd stretch round the Earth 13 times. At 55,800 miles, Canada has the longest coast.

Cliffs being worn down to make sand

? Why are beaches sandy?

Sand is made from tiny fragments of rock and shells, crushed up by the wind and water. Sand is usually yellow or white. But some sand is black because it contains volcanic rock or coal.

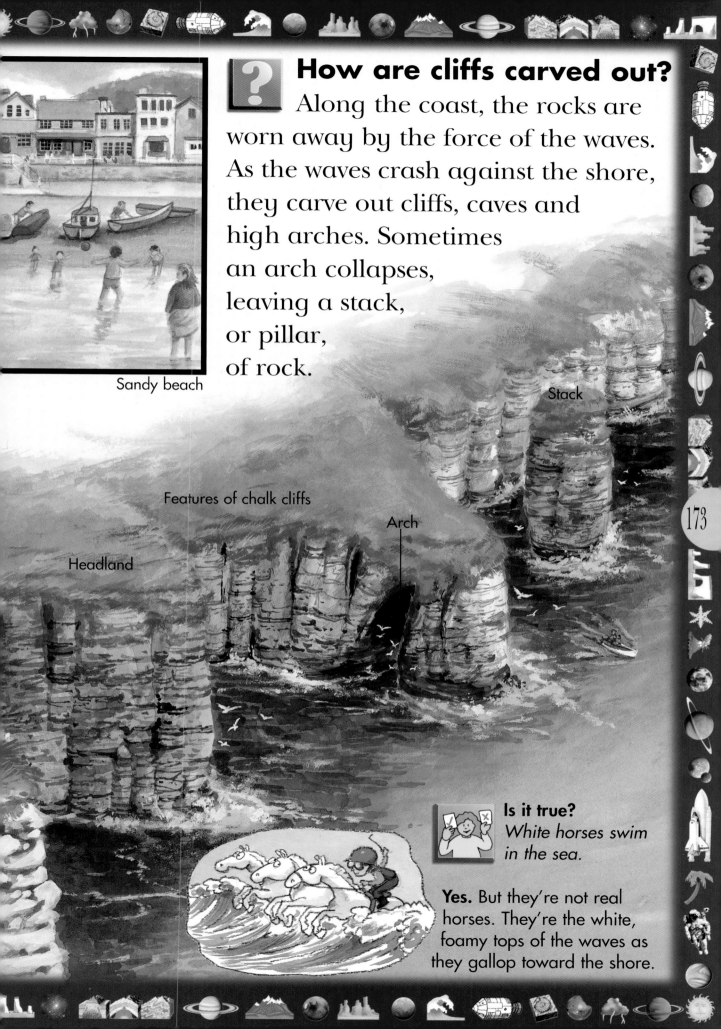

How are cliffs carved out?

Along the coast, the rocks are worn away by the force of the waves. As the waves crash against the shore, they carve out cliffs, caves and high arches. Sometimes an arch collapses, leaving a stack, or pillar, of rock.

Sandy beach

Features of chalk cliffs

Headland

Arch

Stack

173

Is it true?
White horses swim in the sea.

Yes. But they're not real horses. They're the white, foamy tops of the waves as they gallop toward the shore.

How big is the sea?

The sea is absolutely huge! Salty sea water covers about two-thirds of our planet so there's far more sea than land. The sea lies in five oceans – the Pacific, Atlantic, Indian, Arctic and Southern Oceans.

Arctic Ocean

Atlantic Ocean

Indian Ocean

Southern Ocean

Amazing! The first person to set sail around the world was Ferdinand Magellan. He set off from Spain in 1519. Magellan died but one of his ships made it back three years later.

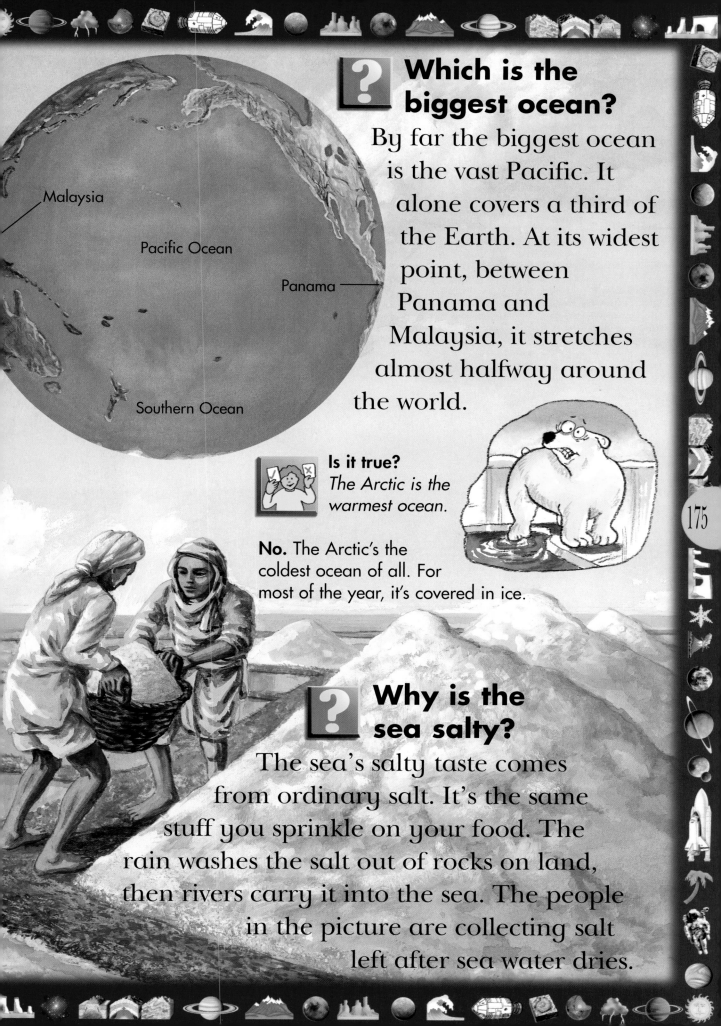

Malaysia

Pacific Ocean

Panama

Southern Ocean

? Which is the biggest ocean?

By far the biggest ocean is the vast Pacific. It alone covers a third of the Earth. At its widest point, between Panama and Malaysia, it stretches almost halfway around the world.

Is it true?
The Arctic is the warmest ocean.

No. The Arctic's the coldest ocean of all. For most of the year, it's covered in ice.

? Why is the sea salty?

The sea's salty taste comes from ordinary salt. It's the same stuff you sprinkle on your food. The rain washes the salt out of rocks on land, then rivers carry it into the sea. The people in the picture are collecting salt left after sea water dries.

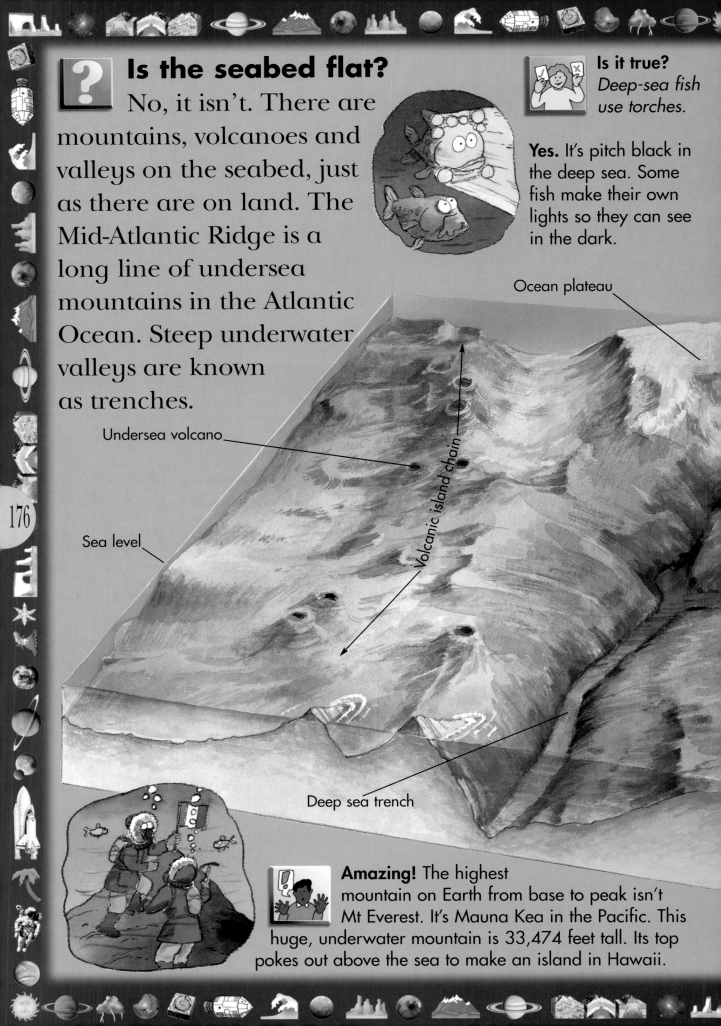

Is the seabed flat?

No, it isn't. There are mountains, volcanoes and valleys on the seabed, just as there are on land. The Mid-Atlantic Ridge is a long line of undersea mountains in the Atlantic Ocean. Steep underwater valleys are known as trenches.

Is it true?
Deep-sea fish use torches.

Yes. It's pitch black in the deep sea. Some fish make their own lights so they can see in the dark.

Ocean plateau

Undersea volcano

Volcanic island chain

Sea level

Deep sea trench

Amazing! The highest mountain on Earth from base to peak isn't Mt Everest. It's Mauna Kea in the Pacific. This huge, underwater mountain is 33,474 feet tall. Its top pokes out above the sea to make an island in Hawaii.

Who builds coral reefs?

Huge coral reefs are built by tiny sea creatures called polyps. The polyps build hard, stony cases around their soft bodies. When they die, the cases are left behind. Millions and millions make a coral reef.

Debris from river

River mouth

Coral reef

Deep sea submersible

Continental shelf

Who dived the deepest?

In 1960, two scientists dived nearly 7 miles into the Marianas Trench in the Pacific Ocean. This is the deepest dive ever made. They traveled in a small submersible called Trieste. It took almost five hours to reach the bottom.

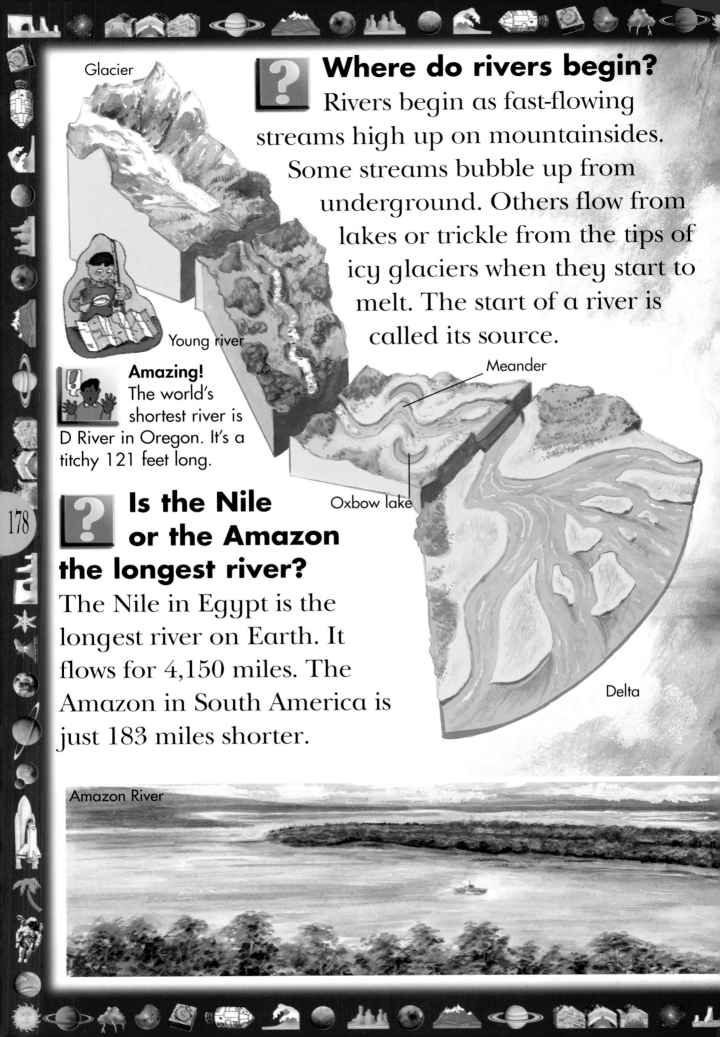

Glacier

Young river

? Where do rivers begin?

Rivers begin as fast-flowing streams high up on mountainsides. Some streams bubble up from underground. Others flow from lakes or trickle from the tips of icy glaciers when they start to melt. The start of a river is called its source.

Meander

Amazing! The world's shortest river is D River in Oregon. It's a titchy 121 feet long.

Oxbow lake

178

? Is the Nile or the Amazon the longest river?

The Nile in Egypt is the longest river on Earth. It flows for 4,150 miles. The Amazon in South America is just 183 miles shorter.

Delta

Amazon River

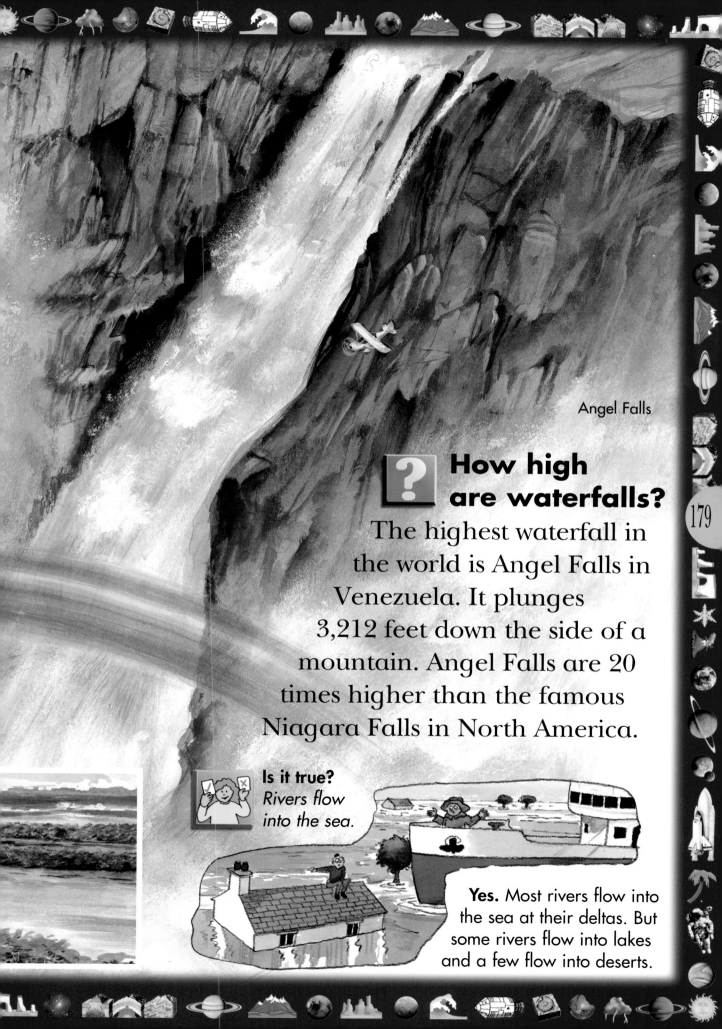

Angel Falls

❓ How high are waterfalls?

179

The highest waterfall in the world is Angel Falls in Venezuela. It plunges 3,212 feet down the side of a mountain. Angel Falls are 20 times higher than the famous Niagara Falls in North America.

Is it true?
Rivers flow into the sea.

Yes. Most rivers flow into the sea at their deltas. But some rivers flow into lakes and a few flow into deserts.

Which lake is the biggest?

The biggest freshwater lake on Earth is Lake Superior in North America. It covers over 51,000 square miles. That's almost as big as the country of Austria. Lake Superior is one of five huge lakes called the Great Lakes.

Great Lakes

Lake Superior

Is it true?
There's a monster in Loch Ness.

Maybe. Some people say Nessie is a type of prehistoric reptile that lives in the Scottish lake. Others say this is nonsense. What do you think?

Volcanic lake

Oxbow lake

Amazing! The Dead Sea in the Middle East is so salty, you can float on the surface. No fish can live in it.

Lake Titicaca

Where is the highest lake?

Lake Titicaca in South America is the highest lake on which boats can sail. It's 12,500 feet up in the Andes Mountains. People who live around the lake build boats from lake reeds.

Tarn

Glacial lake

River basin lake

How are lakes made?

Some lakes formed long ago, in hollows scraped out by ice. These filled with water as the ice melted. Some lakes form in the tops of volcanoes or when a river cuts through a bend.

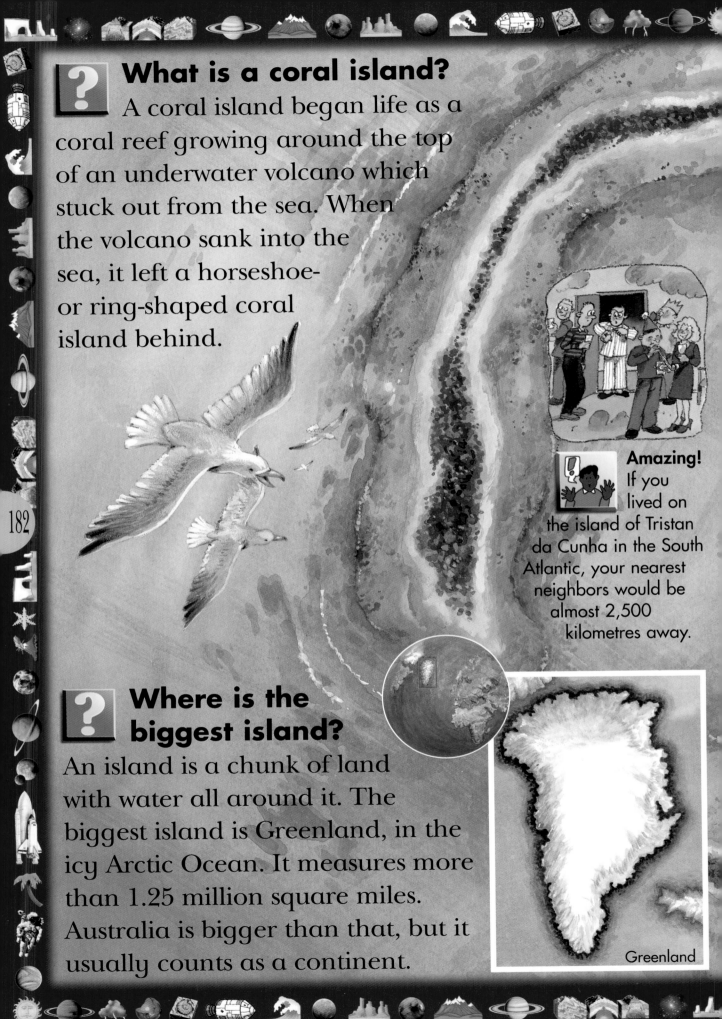

? What is a coral island?

A coral island began life as a coral reef growing around the top of an underwater volcano which stuck out from the sea. When the volcano sank into the sea, it left a horseshoe- or ring-shaped coral island behind.

Amazing! If you lived on the island of Tristan da Cunha in the South Atlantic, your nearest neighbors would be almost 2,500 kilometres away.

? Where is the biggest island?

An island is a chunk of land with water all around it. The biggest island is Greenland, in the icy Arctic Ocean. It measures more than 1.25 million square miles. Australia is bigger than that, but it usually counts as a continent.

Greenland

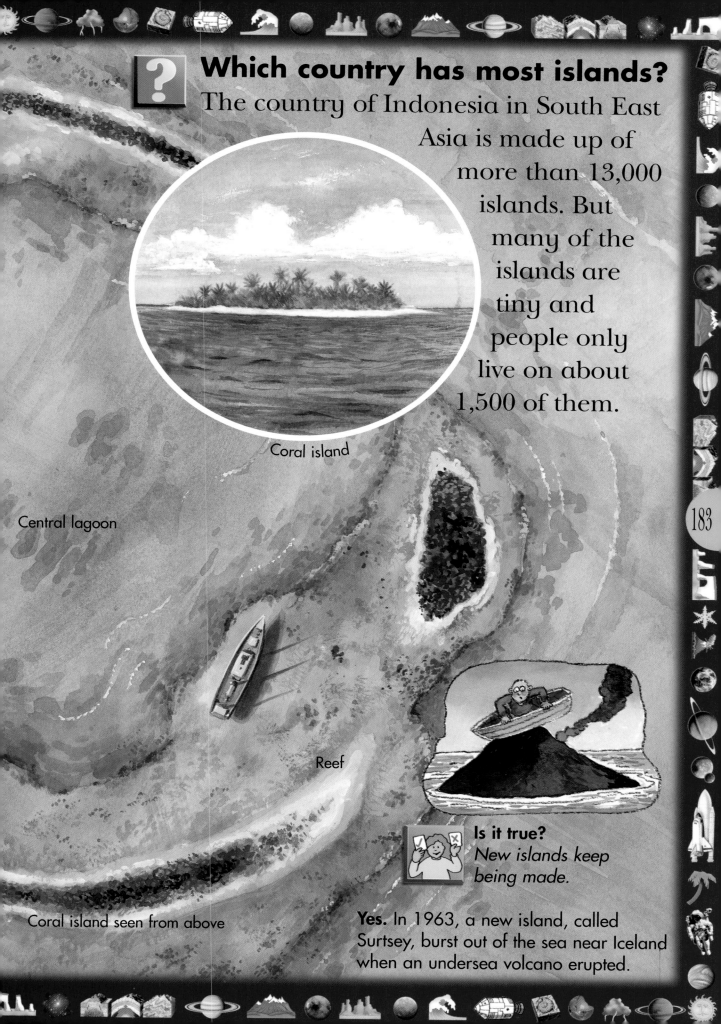

? Which country has most islands?

The country of Indonesia in South East Asia is made up of more than 13,000 islands. But many of the islands are tiny and people only live on about 1,500 of them.

Coral island

Central lagoon

183

Reef

Coral island seen from above

Is it true?
New islands keep being made.

Yes. In 1963, a new island, called Surtsey, burst out of the sea near Iceland when an undersea volcano erupted.

Why are deserts dry?

Deserts are the driest places on Earth. In some deserts it doesn't rain for years at a time. In others, it never rains at all. Some deserts are also scorching hot. In the daytime, the sand's hot enough to fry an egg on.

Sandy desert seen from above

Amazing! The Sahara Desert is the biggest, sandiest desert in the world. It covers about a third of Africa.

Can sand dunes move?

Strong winds blowing across the desert pile the sand up into giant heaps, or dunes. The biggest stand 650 feet tall. The dunes creep forward every year and can bury whole desert villages.

Sand dunes covering a town

Mesa

Butte

Sand dunes

Salt lake

Dried salt flat

Rocky desert

Volcanic desert

Desert landscapes

? Are all deserts sandy?

No, they're not. Only about a quarter of all deserts are sandy. Most deserts are rocky or covered in gravel and stones. Some deserts have high mountains or strange-shaped rocks towering up from the ground.

Is it true?
Mushrooms grow in the desert.

Yes. Well, mushroom-shaped rocks. They're carved into shape by sand blown by the wind, like a giant piece of sandpaper.

? **Why are rainforests so wet?**

Because it rains almost every single day! Late most afternoons, the sky goes black and there's a heavy thunderstorm. Rainforests grow along the equator where it's hot and sticky all year round. It's the perfect weather for plants to grow.

Rainforest

Coniferous forest

? Where do the biggest forests grow?

The biggest forests in the world stretch for thousands of miles across the north of Europe and Asia. The trees that grow here are conifers. They're trees with needle-like leaves and cones.

Is it true? *The paper we use comes from forests.*

Yes. You could make more than 1,500 copies of this book from a single conifer tree.

Amazing! The biggest rainforest grows in South America along the banks of the River Amazon. It's home to millions of plants and animals.

187

Rainforest layers

Emergent layer

Canopy layer

Understorey

Ground layer

? How do rainforests grow?

Rainforests grow in layers depending on the height of the trees. The tallest trees poke out above the forest. Below them is a thick roof of tree-tops called the canopy. Next comes a layer of shorter trees, herbs and shrubs.

African savannah (grassland)

❓ What are grasslands?

Grasslands are huge plains of grass, trees and bushes. They grow in warm, dry places where there's too little rain for forests to grow, but enough rain to stop the land turning into a desert.

South American gauchos farming on grassland

? Why did a grassland turn to dust?

In the 1930s, farmers in the south-west USA plowed up the grasslands to grow wheat. But a terrible drought turned the soil to dry, useless dust which blew away in the wind. This was called a dustbowl.

Amazing! Grassland animals eat different bits of the grass to avoid competition – zebras eat the tops, wildebeest eat the stems.

Dustbowl

? What are grasslands used for?

People use grasslands for grazing animals such as cattle which are raised for their meat. They also grow crops such as wheat and barley in gigantic fields. One wheat field in Canada was the size of 20,000 football fields.

Is it true?
Rice is a type of grass.

Yes. Rice is a cereal plant, which belongs to the grass family. The grains of rice come from the flower-heads. Rice grows in flooded fields in South East Asia.

CHAPTER SEVEN

VIOLENT EARTH

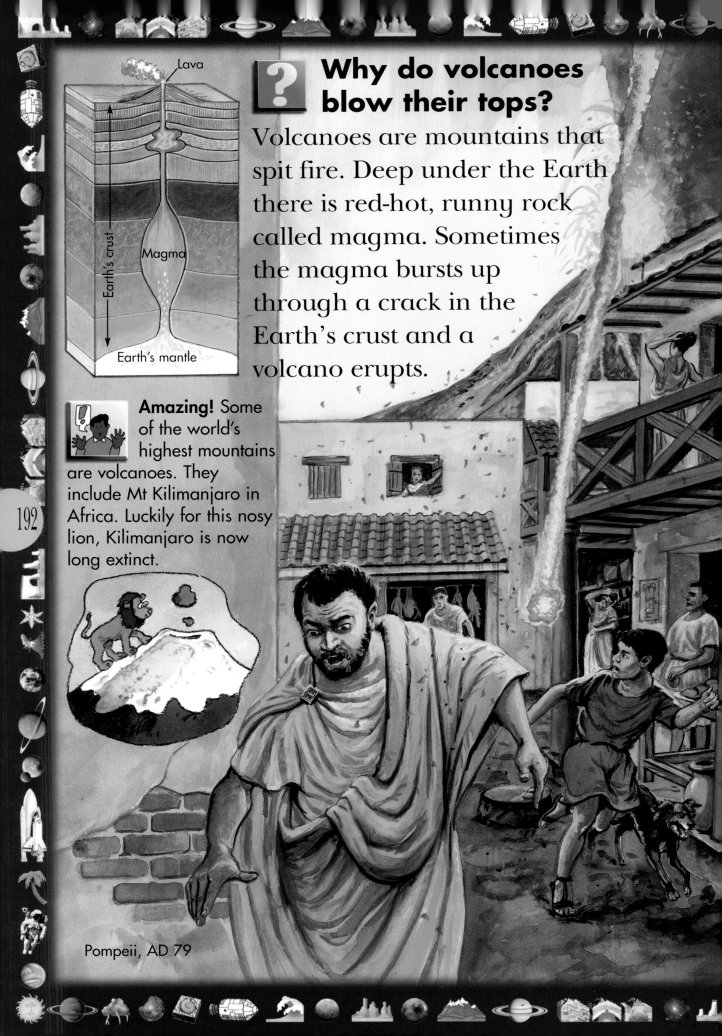

Lava

Earth's crust

Magma

Earth's mantle

? Why do volcanoes blow their tops?

Volcanoes are mountains that spit fire. Deep under the Earth there is red-hot, runny rock called magma. Sometimes the magma bursts up through a crack in the Earth's crust and a volcano erupts.

Amazing! Some of the world's highest mountains are volcanoes. They include Mt Kilimanjaro in Africa. Luckily for this nosy lion, Kilimanjaro is now long extinct.

192

Pompeii, AD 79

Volcano erupting

? What is lava?

Once magma has erupted from a volcano, it is called lava. Some lava is thick and lumpy. Some is thin and runny. In the air, it cools and turns into hard, black rock.

Is it true?
Volcanic ash can flow as fast as a train.

Yes. Clouds of gas and ash can flow across the ground at 100 mph!

? What happened to Pompeii?

In AD 79, Mt Vesuvius in Italy blew its top in a massive explosion. The nearby city of Pompeii was buried under a huge cloud of hot ash and rock. Thousands of people were suffocated. Others fled for their lives.

Mt St Helen's, USA was a dormant volcano that erupted.

? How long do volcanoes sleep for?

Hundreds or even thousands of years.
A sleeping volcano is called dormant.
But it can wake up at any minute.
A volcano that still erupts is called
active. An extinct volcano is one that
is never likely to erupt again.

Geyser in Yellowstone Park, Wyoming

Amazing! The most active volcano
on Earth is Kilauea in Hawaii. It
has erupted non-stop for almost
20 years! All that lava means the island of
Hawaii is getting bigger, every day.

Why do people live near volcanoes?

Despite the danger, many people all over the world live near volcanoes. The ash that explodes out of a volcano makes the soil very rich for growing crops. People also use volcanic rock for building.

Is it true?
You only get volcanoes on land.

No. There are hundreds of volcanoes on land and many more under the sea. Some poke out above the surface to form islands, such as Hawaii.

Town covered in ash after eruption of Mt Pinatubo, Philippines

Why do geysers gush?

Geysers are giant jets of scalding water and steam. They happen in places with lots of volcanoes. The red-hot rocks underground heat water far below the surface until it's so hot it shoots through a crack.

Fault runs through Earth's crust.

Crust tries to move.

Pressure builds up.

Earthquake finally occurs as pieces move apart with a jerk.

? What makes the Earth shake?

The Earth's surface is cracked into enormous pieces which drift on the red-hot, runny rock below. Sometimes two pieces push and shove each other, making the Earth shake.

Kobe earthquake, Japan, 1995

? How much damage do earthquakes cause?

Big earthquakes do lots of damage. Huge cracks open up in the ground. Houses, roads and bridges shake and fall down. In the worst earthquakes, many people are killed and injured by buildings that collapse on top of them.

Seismograph
(earthquake measuring device)

❓ How do scientists measure an earthquake?

An earthquake sends shock waves rippling through the ground. Scientists study these waves to see how big the earthquake is. They measure earthquakes on a scale of 1 to 10. Each quake on the scale is 30 times worse than the one before.

Is it true?
People used to think earthquakes were caused by fish.

Yes. In Japan, people thought quakes were caused by a giant catfish wriggling about on the seabed. The gods had to put a rock on the fish's head to make it stay still!

? What is a tsunami?

Tsunamis are gigantic waves which can be 100 feet high and 125 miles long. The word tsunami means "harbor wave" in Japanese because of the way the waves crash into the harbor. They are also called tidal waves.

Is it true?
The biggest tsunami was as tall as the Statue of Liberty.

Yes. This whopping wave was 280 feet high, almost as tall as the Statue of Liberty. It swept past Japan in 1971.

Amazing! A tsunami can travel across the sea at high speed. Some race along at 550 mph. That's as fast as a jet plane. The deeper the water, the faster they flow.

Earthquake at sea creates fast waves.

Wave gets taller near land.

❓ How do tsunamis start?

Tsunamis are triggered by volcanoes or earthquakes under the sea. At first, the waves are low as they speed across the sea. As they reach land, the water piles up into a massive wave which crashes down on to the shore.

Tsunamis can leave boats stranded inland.

❓ What happens when a tsunami hits land?

When a tsunami hits land, watch out! It smashes down on to the shore, washing houses, people and boats away. A tsunami can sweep a boat into the air and dump it far away.

How do floods happen?

Many floods happen when it rains very heavily and rivers overflow. They burst their banks and flood the land all around. You also get floods in stormy weather when high tides or gigantic waves sweep on to the shore.

Flash flood of Ouvèze River, France

Amazing! The Thames Barrier was finished in 1984 to stop the River Thames flooding and drowning London, England. Ten huge steel gates swing up to make a massive dam.

What are flash floods?

Flash floods are floods that happen very suddenly, with no warning. Sometimes there isn't time to evacuate buildings in the flood's path. Flash floods can happen in the desert too, during a rare rainstorm.

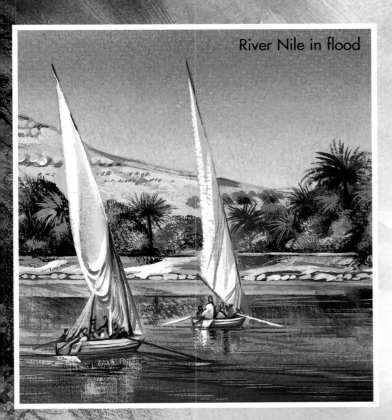

River Nile in flood

Is it true?
Floods can wash whole buildings away.

Yes. In 1955, a flood in the USA washed a four-storey wooden hotel clean away. Imagine how surprised the guests were when they looked out of their windows!

201

Are some floods useful?

Yes, they are. The River Nile in Egypt used to flood every year, leaving rich mud on the fields. The mud made the soil ideal for farmers to grow bumper crops. The Nile doesn't flood any more because a large dam was built to store its water.

The Mississippi River flooded 50,000 square miles, in 1993.

When do thunderstorms happen?

Thunderstorms usually happen on a hot, summer's day when the air is warm and sticky. Watch out for huge, dark, tall thunderclouds gathering in the sky. They're a sure sign a storm's brewing. Time to head indoors!

What makes thunder rumble?

Lightning is incredibly hot, about five times hotter than the Sun's surface. As it streaks through the sky, it heats the air so quickly that it makes a loud booming sound. This is the sound of thunder.

Where do thunderstorms begin?

Thunder starts in cumulonimbus clouds. They turn the sky purply black and blue. Some of these clouds are massive. The tallest can grow 11 miles high. That's more than twice the height of Mt Everest.

Cumulonimbus thundercloud

Is it true?
Lightning happens before thunder.

No. They happen at exactly the same time. But you see lightning before you hear thunder because light travels more quickly than sound.

Amazing! The Vikings believed that thunder was caused by the bad-tempered god, Thor, hurling his hammer across the sky.

? What makes lightning flash?

Inside a thundercloud, strong winds hurl drops of water around. They bump and bash into each other. This makes the cloud crackle with static electricity which builds up and suddenly streaks through the sky as lightning. Lightning can flash inside clouds or from cloud to ground.

Empire State Building, New York City, during thunderstorm

? Does lightning ever strike twice?

Yes, it does. The Empire State Building is struck about 500 times a year! Many tall buildings, such as churches and skyscrapers, have lightning conductors to carry the electricity of the lightning safely away.

? What is ball lightning?

Lightning comes in different shapes, such as forked, sheet and ribbon lightning. Ball lightning looks like a ball of fire. People have seen balls of lightning float into their house, then explode with a bang.

Amazing! Park ranger, Roy C. Sullivan, was struck by lightning a record seven times. He suffered burns, singed hair and eyebrows, and he even lost his toenails!

There are many stories of ball lightning entering houses.

Is it true?
Lightning takes the slowest path to the ground.

No. It takes the quickest. That's why you should never shelter under a tall tree during a storm. If the lightning strikes the tree, you might get fried.

? Where do avalanches strike?

Avalanches strike on snow-covered mountainsides. A huge slab of snow and ice suddenly breaks loose and crashes downhill. Avalanches can slide at speeds of up to 200 mph, as fast as a racing car, as hundreds of tons of snow hurtle down the slope.

Sniffer dogs search for buried victims.

? Can people survive avalanches?

Avalanches are deadly. They can bury people, cars and whole villages in their path. Victims suffocate under the snow unless they're rescued quickly. Rescue teams use specially trained dogs to sniff survivors out.

 Amazing! In World War I, soldiers fighting each other in the Alps used avalanches as weapons. They fired guns at the mountainsides to set off killer avalanches.

Is it true?
Yodeling can set off an avalanche.

Yes. In some Swiss mountain villages yodeling is banned in spring in case it sets an avalanche off. You're not allowed to shout or sing loudly either, in case the vibrations of sound waves in the air shake and loosen the snow, to start an avalanche.

? What sets off an avalanche?

If the snow gets too heavy, it can suddenly start to slip and slide. But other things can trigger an avalanche. A skier, or even a car door being slammed can set the snow sliding.

Weight of snow creates cracks, and a large chunk slips away.

Layers of snow and ice build up on mountainside.

? Why are blizzards dangerous?

A blizzard is a snowstorm. Strong winds blow the snow into drifts and it can be difficult to see. A blizzard can bring a busy city to a standstill. People and traffic can't move about, and schools and offices have to be closed.

Amazing! You don't only get snow in cold places. In 1981, snow fell in the Kalahari Desert in Africa for the first time in living memory. The temperature dropped to a chilly minus 5°C.

? Which is the snowiest place?

The snowiest place in the world is Mt Rainier in Washington. In one year, snow 100 feet deep fell there. That's enough snow to build a snowman as tall as 17 people. Fancy having a go?

What is a hailstone made from?

A hailstone is a small ball of ice that starts life in a thundercloud. Inside the cloud, a chip of ice is tossed up and down many times. It gets coated in layers of ice, just like the layers of an onion.

Build-up of a hailstone within a thundercloud

Cross-section of a hailstone, showing the layers of ice

Is it true?
The biggest hailstone was the size of a peach.

No. It was bigger than that! Hailstones are usually the size of peas but the biggest was the size of a watermelon. It fell in Kansas, in 1970.

Record-breaking hailstone

What are hurricanes?

Hurricanes are giant storms that begin over warm tropical seas. They are like huge spinning wheels of wind, rain and clouds. They sweep across the sea, then begin to die down when they reach land.

Cross-section of a hurricane

Eye

Rain

An Atlantic hurricane hits the island of Antigua.

Is it true?
Hurricanes have names.

Yes. Hurricanes are given names from an alphabetical list. A new list is made every year. The names of the worst hurricanes, like Andrew or Carol, are never used again.

Andrew

Carol

How big are hurricanes?

Hurricanes can be enormous. Some measure 1,800 miles across and even the smallest are about the size of Florida. Winds inside a hurricane can blow at over 180 mph.

Amazing! If you could collect the energy inside a hurricane for one day and turn it into electricity, it would run the whole USA for six months.

Hurricanes can even pick up and dump airplanes.

Eye of hurricane seen from space

Do hurricanes have eyes?

Yes, they do. The eye is a patch of calm, clear weather in the hurricane's center. As the eye passes over land, there's a break in the storm for an hour or so. Then it begins again.

❓ What makes a tornado twist?

A tornado is a fierce, twisting wind which hangs from a thundercloud. It starts when wind inside the cloud starts to spin very quickly. A twisty tornado speeds across the ground, sucking up everything in its way.

Storm chasers observing a tornado in Kansas

Amazing! Some people track tornadoes for fun. They drive as close to the twister as they dare, then take video films and photographs. It's a very dangerous hobby!

A tornado leaving a trail of damage

Is it true?
Tornadoes can pick up trains.

Yes. In 1931, a tornado in Minnesota picked a train clean off its tracks and dumped it in a ditch. Tornadoes often pick up cars and cows!

How quickly do tornadoes travel?

Most tornadoes travel at about 18 mph, but some are much speedier movers. They race along the ground as quickly as a car. What's more, the wind inside a tornado can blow at an amazing 300 mph.

Do tornadoes happen at sea?

Yes, they're called waterspouts. These giant twists of water can be a mile tall. In the past, sailors thought waterspouts were sea monsters!

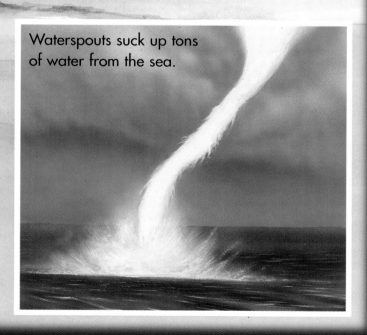

Waterspouts suck up tons of water from the sea.

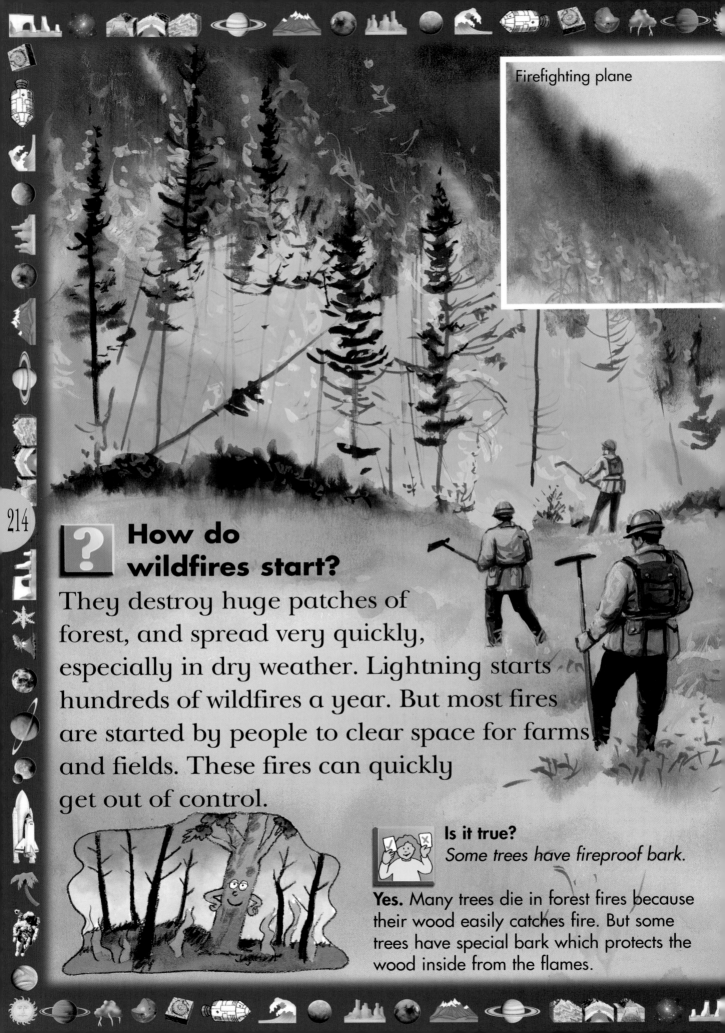

Firefighting plane

? How do wildfires start?

They destroy huge patches of forest, and spread very quickly, especially in dry weather. Lightning starts hundreds of wildfires a year. But most fires are started by people to clear space for farms and fields. These fires can quickly get out of control.

Is it true?
Some trees have fireproof bark.

Yes. Many trees die in forest fires because their wood easily catches fire. But some trees have special bark which protects the wood inside from the flames.

? How do people fight wildfires?

Fighting a wildfire is difficult and dangerous. Special planes fly overhead spraying the forest with millions of gallons of water. Firefighters on the ground try to hold back the fire with water and beaters.

Firefighters battle a large wildfire.

? What is a heatwave?

A heatwave is very hot weather which lasts much longer than usual. The scorching heat can kill people, animals and crops. It also dries up reservoirs, and melts the surface of roads.

Duststorm during the Midwest heatwave, 1937

Amazing! It can take hundreds of years for a forest to grow again after a fire. But sometimes fires can be good for forests. They clear space for new plants to grow.

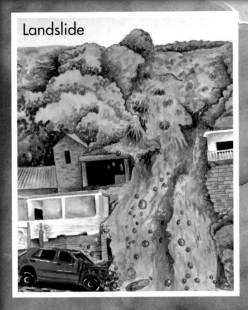
Landslide

? What makes the land slide?

A landslide is a huge fall of soil or mud which suddenly breaks off a cliff or mountainside and slides downhill. Some landslides are caused by volcanoes, heavy rain, or earthquakes, which make the ground shake and slip.

? Where was the worst mudslide?

The worst mudslide happened in Colombia, South America. In 1985, a volcano erupted and melted masses of snow and ice, turning the soil to mud. The mud poured downhill at top speed and buried a whole town.

AERO EXPRESO BOGAT

Mudslide survivors are rescued by helicopter in Armero, Colombia.

Why do cliffs collapse?

As the waves crash against a cliff, they wear the bottom of the cliff away. If the cliff becomes too top-heavy, it collapses into the sea. Along the east coast of England, whole cliff-top villages have toppled into the sea.

Is it true?
Cutting down trees causes landslides.

Yes. Tree roots are useful for sticking the soil together. If the trees are cut down, the soil turns to mud and washes away when it rains.

Cliff collapsing into the sea

Amazing! Mudslides can slide at high speeds of up to 70 mph. They can slither along for as much as 60 miles before coming to a stop.

217

El Niño is represented by the red areas along the center of the Earth.

❓ What is El Niño?

El Niño is a warm band of water which flows in the sea along the coast of South America. Scientists blame El Niño for changing the weather, by causing more storms, floods, droughts and tornadoes every few years.

Is it true?
It can rain cats and dogs.

No. But you can get showers of fish, frogs, flowers, coal, nuts and even maggots! Scientists think the wind scoops them up, then they fall again in the rain.

What are monsoons?

Monsoons are winds that bring heavy rain to tropical places such as India and South East Asia, during the summer months. Farmers rely on this rain to water their crops, because during the cooler months, there might be little or no rainfall.

 Amazing! A turtle once fell in a hailstone in the USA. It had somehow been sucked up into a thundercloud and covered in layers of ice.

The monsoon season can bring severe flooding.

What is a sandstorm?

A sandstorm is a thick, choking cloud of sand whipped up by the wind in the desert. If you get caught in a sandstorm the best thing to do is cover your nose and mouth. Then you won't breathe the choking sand in.

219

Sandstorm in Africa

CHAPTER EIGHT

OUR EARTH

? Is Earth a healthy planet?

Look at Earth from space and you see a mainly blue, watery planet with swirling white clouds. All looks well, but get closer, and you see a different picture. Parts of Earth are unhealthy – and all because of the way we live.

Earth seen from space

? Does Earth need looking after?

Earth is our only home – we can't live on other planets. We need to look after it to make sure it stays a beautiful, healthy place. If we don't care for the Earth now, we will spoil it for the people of the future.

Can I help care for the Earth?

There are many things you can do in your everyday life to care for the Earth. This book tells you about some of them. Just think, if everyone did the same as you, Earth would be a better place to live.

Our Solar System has nine planets that orbit the Sun.

Is it true?
There is no other planet like Earth.

Yes. There is only one Earth. It is special – it is the only planet known to have life on it. Perhaps one day life will be found on another planet, too.

Amazing! There has been life on Earth for approximately 3.5 billion years.

? **Is Earth's climate changing?**

Earth's climate is slowly getting warmer. Scientists who study the climate have found that it is a little warmer now than it was 100 years ago. You may not notice the difference, but plants and animals do.

Climate study in the Antarctic

Is it true?
Trees reduce carbon dioxide in the atmosphere.

Yes. Tree leaves take harmful carbon dioxide from the atmosphere and give out oxygen. We breathe the oxygen they make.

Cars and factories burn "fossil fuels" which produce harmful "greenhouse gases."

Why is the temperature rising?

It's getting warmer because of what the Earth's 6 billion people are doing. Because of the way we lead our lives, we are changing the Earth's climate. We are making the planet grow warmer.

Amazing! There is far more carbon dioxide in the atmosphere than there was 200 years ago. This is mainly why it's warmer today than it was in the past.

How are we making the temperature rise?

By burning "fossil fuels" – coal, oil and natural gas – we are putting "greenhouse gases," such as carbon dioxide, into the atmosphere. The gases surround the Earth and keep heat in.

? What will happen as the temperature rises?

As the Earth's climate warms up, glaciers and the ice at the North and South Poles will melt, causing the sea level to rise. This will bring floods, and some islands will disappear. Deserts will spread, and droughts will occur.

226

Amazing! Cows are making the temperature rise. The smelly greenhouse gas methane comes from animals, such as cows, and from factories. Humans make it, too!

How can governments reduce carbon dioxide levels?

Burning gasoline in cars puts carbon dioxide into the atmosphere. Governments can build transport systems that don't make carbon dioxide, and order more trees to be planted.

Electric railway

What can I do to help?

Use less electricity. This is because most electricity comes from burning fossil fuels which makes carbon dioxide. Switch off lights, TVs and computers when not in use.

Is it true?
If the Antarctic ice sheet melted, the sea level would rise.

Yes. It holds two-thirds of the Earth's fresh water. If it melted, the sea would rise by up to 230 feet. Coastlines would change all over the world.

Antarctica

? What other problems are caused by burning fossil fuels?

Sulphur dioxide is another harmful gas that comes from power stations and vehicles. It is very acidic, which means it eats things away. In the atmosphere, it mixes with droplets of moisture to make acid rain. Trees die when acid rain falls on them and on their soil.

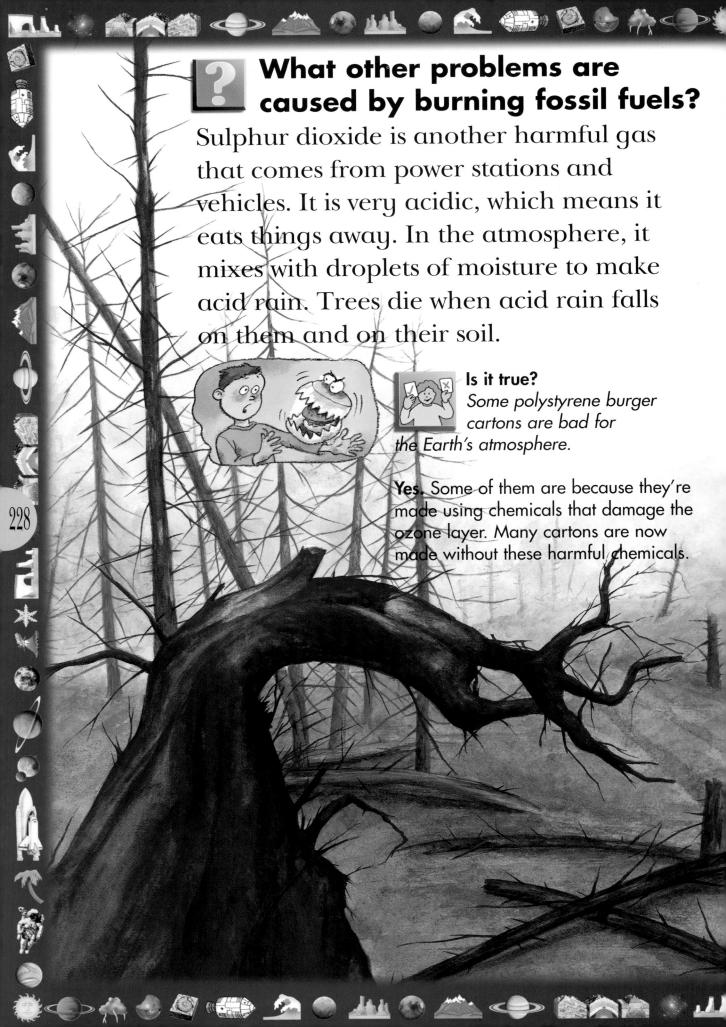

Is it true?
Some polystyrene burger cartons are bad for the Earth's atmosphere.

Yes. Some of them are because they're made using chemicals that damage the ozone layer. Many cartons are now made without these harmful chemicals.

Is Earth's atmosphere being harmed?

There is a layer of helpful gas around the Earth called ozone. It protects us from the Sun's dangerous ultraviolet rays. Unfortunately, the ozone layer is damaged because humans have put harmful chemicals into the atmosphere.

WARNING! Always use a sunscreen in sunny weather to protect your skin from the Sun's rays.

Amazing! When a nuclear power station at Chernobyl, Ukraine, exploded in 1986, radioactive material was sent into the atmosphere. Animals across Europe were contaminated by the radiation.

Scandinavian forest damaged by acid rain

Underground storage of nuclear waste

Is nuclear power dangerous?

Nuclear power stations do not burn fossil fuels. Therefore, they do not make harmful gases. But they do make radioactive waste material. It is dangerous and will have to be guarded for many years into the future.

? Are there alternatives to fossil fuels?

There are other ways to make power. Solar panels collect energy from the Sun. The spinning propellers of wind turbines collect energy from the wind. Each of these energy-collectors makes electricity.

Amazing! Cars can be powered by all sorts of things – solar power, natural gas, and even chicken droppings!

Wind turbines convert energy from the wind into electricity.

❓ Are there any other types of natural fuel?

In many countries small amounts of energy come from rotting plants and animal dung. The methane they give off is burned to provide light and heat. This type of fuel is called bio-gas.

Bio-gas plant in India

❓ Are these fuels better for the Earth?

Yes, they are. Solar power, wind power and bio-gas are cleaner, or "green," forms of energy. They don't make harmful gases. They don't pollute the atmosphere. They don't make acid rain. They don't harm the ozone layer.

231

Is it true?
Electricity can be made from water.

Yes. Running water is used to make electricity. This is hydroelectric power. The electricity is made by power stations built in or near dams.

Hoover Dam, Arizona

? Are animals in danger?

Thousands of different animals live on Earth. It is their planet, as well as ours. Sadly, because of what we do, many animals are in danger. An oil spill at sea harms seals, birds and fish. When forests are cut down, many animals lose their homes.

Oil spill

? How many kinds of animals are in danger?

There are many thousands of different kinds of animals in danger. Some are so rare they are endangered. This means they are almost extinct – they have almost died out. If that happens, they will have gone forever.

Endangered species

What is being done to save animals?

Many endangered animals are now protected by law. It is wrong for people to harm them, or the places where they live. Some endangered animals are bred in zoos. This helps to increase their numbers.

Golden lion tamarin

Is it true?
Humans are causing animals to die out.

Yes. It's said that one kind of animal dies out every 30 minutes because of what we're doing to the planet.

Amazing! Passenger pigeons used to form flocks of millions of birds, but they were hunted to extinction in the wild. The very last one, named Martha, died in 1914.

Cormorant covered in oil

? Why do people kill certain animals?

Animals are killed for lots of reasons. Birds are killed for their colorful feathers. Elephants are hunted for their ivory. Tigers are killed for their skins. It's against the law, but it still goes on.

Stuffed animals

Amazing! Every year around 100 million animals and plants are taken without permission from the wild. It is because of this that they are endangered.

Collecting rainforest plants

What about plants?

Like animals, plants can die out too. More than 30,000 different kinds of plants are in danger all over the world. Collectors take them from the wild, or pay local people to do it for them.

235

Is it true?
Sea turtles are hunted for their shells.

Yes. Even though it's illegal, sea turtle shell, called tortoiseshell, is still used to make spectacle frames and souvenirs for tourists.

What can I do to help?

Don't buy goods made from ivory, fur, coral or tortoiseshell. Don't pick or dig up wild plants. If you eat tuna fish, make sure it's dolphin-friendly. Dolphins die in some fishing nets.

Illegal animal goods

Why are forests good for the Earth?

Forests are the "lungs" of the planet. Their trees make much of the oxygen we breathe. Forests provide us with food and timber. Some medicines are made from plants found only in forests.

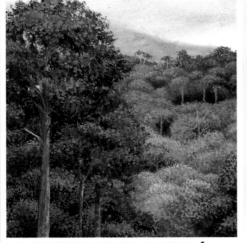
Rainforest

Are forests in danger?

Forests are in danger in many parts of the world. In some countries trees are killed by acid rain. Elsewhere, whole forests are cut down for their timber, or to make way for farm land.

Logger truck

What is being done to save forests?

Some governments have stopped cutting down the forests on their land. Many forests that are left are protected by law. Also, new forests are being planted, to grow timber like any other crop. It is grown to be cut down.

Amazing! Since 1980, an area of tropical forest six times the size of France has been turned into farm land, or plantations of oil palm, rubber and other crops.

Is it true?
Soil erosion can be seen from space.

Yes. Trees keep soil in place. Where forests are cleared the soil wears away, or erodes, until only rock is left.

237

Soil erosion on Madagascar, seen from space

How much trash do people make?

Too much! People make trash and every household makes lots of it every day. In Britain, every family makes about 3.85 pounds of trash each day. Over one year that adds up to more than half a ton of trash!

Is it true?
Some garbage is dumped at sea.

Yes. Every day thousands of tons of garbage are thrown into the sea. The seabed is littered with garbage, such as bits of plastic, that never rot away.

Garbage dump

Garbage dumped at sea

238

What happens to all this trash?

Because so much trash is made, it's a problem to deal with it all. Some is burned inside furnaces. A lot is buried on the land. Some garbage is collected and sent for recycling.

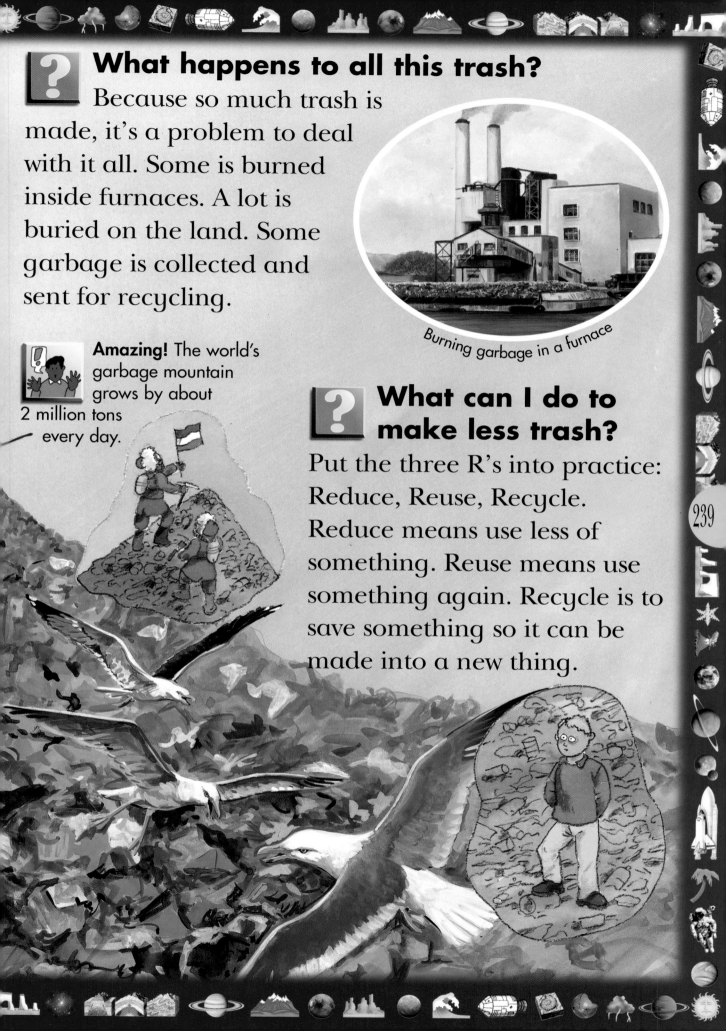

Burning garbage in a furnace

Amazing! The world's garbage mountain grows by about 2 million tons every day.

What can I do to make less trash?

Put the three R's into practice: Reduce, Reuse, Recycle. Reduce means use less of something. Reuse means use something again. Recycle is to save something so it can be made into a new thing.

What can I do with glass?

When glass bottles and jars are empty, wash them out and take them to a bottle bank. Most supermarkets have bottle banks. When the banks are full, the glass goes to a factory. It is crushed, melted and made into new bottles and jars.

Amazing! Around 6 billion glass bottles and jars are used in Britain every year, but only three out of every ten are recycled.

Bottle bank

What can I do with plastic?

Some kinds of plastic can be recycled. Plastic bottles for fizzy drinks are often made of recyclable plastic. It can be turned into material to make plastic parts for cars. These bottles can also be reused, by making them into useful items.

Reused plastic bottles

Paper recycling

What can I do with paper?

Most paper can be recycled, from newspapers and phone books to candy wrappers and envelopes. It is made into new paper and cardboard.

241

Is it true?
Glass can be recycled over and over again.

Yes. You just keep on crushing it, melting it and making it into new bottles and jars.

? What can I do with aluminum cans?

Cans that hold fizzy drinks and even sardines are often made from a lightweight metal called aluminum. Look for the ALU symbol on them. They can be melted down and made into new cans.

Can recycling

Reusing clothes

Amazing! In Britain they throw away around 11 million aluminum cans every day. If you think that's a lot, the USA throws out 200 million!

❓ What can I do with steel cans?

Most food cans are made from steel. A magnet will stick to a steel can. If it doesn't stick, the can is probably made from aluminum. Wash the cans out and take them to a can bank. Steel is the world's most recycled material.

Using magnets to test cans

❓ What can I do with old clothes?

Give old clothes to charity shops. They are sorted out and many are sold as second-hand clothes. Some old clothes are sent abroad. Tatty clothes are sent to textile mills where they are ripped to pieces and used to make felt.

Is it true?
Christmas trees can be recycled.

Yes. Real Christmas trees (not plastic ones!) can be cut into tiny pieces, called chippings, which are used by gardeners.

243

? What can I do with kitchen and garden waste?

Vegetable peel, tea leaves and grass cuttings are "green" waste. If you pile them into a heap in the garden, they will rot down to make compost.

Even some kinds of paper can be turned into compost.

? Why is compost good for the environment?

Compost is food for the soil. It contains nutrients (foods) that keep soil healthy. Using home-made compost means less peat compost is dug up from natural places, and animals' homes are saved.

Gardening with compost

❓ Are there other ways of recycling green waste?

You don't need a garden to recycle green waste! You can make small amounts of compost and plant food inside a wormery – a container where a colony of worms live. Worm bins can be kept inside or outside.

Is it true?
Leaves make good compost.

Yes. Leaves rot down slowly to become leaf mold. Put them in a black bag or an open-topped wire cage. After two years you'll have compost.

Amazing! Green waste in a garbage dump makes dangerous methane gas, and liquid that can pollute water and kill wildlife. It's safer to make it into compost.

Polluted river

245

Are there any dangers to our food?

Some people are worried about genetically modified (GM) foods, where the genes – instructions – have been changed by scientists. Because this has not happened in nature, no one knows how safe these foods are.

Amazing! Pollen from crops that have had their genes changed can mix with organically grown crops. When this happens, an organic crop is no longer organic.

Organic farm of the past

What does "organic farming" mean?

It's a natural way of farming where crops are grown and animals raised without using man-made chemicals. Also, the plants and animals have not been changed in any way.

Spraying crops with chemicals can harm the delicate balance of nature.

Is it true?
GM crops need fewer pesticides.

Yes. Scientists are changing the genes inside some crops so that they can resist diseases and pests on their own.

What can I do about it?
It's easy, and fun, to grow some foods at home, such as cress and tomatoes. Be organic, so don't put any chemicals on them. They'll taste good!

Tomato growing

What can I do at home?

Inside the house, start your own recycling center, collecting materials that can be recycled. Reuse plastic bags, switch off electrical items when they're not in use, and don't leave faucets dripping. Outside, get composting, and grow your own organic vegetables.

Amazing! Even an alien would think Earth needs caring for. That's because there are 100,000 pieces of space junk whizzing around the planet.

Energy-efficient house

Insulation to keep the heat in.

Switch off electrical items after use.

Don't leave faucets dripping.

Cycling is energy-efficient and good exercise.

Grow your own organic vegetables.

Green Club

 What can I do at school?

If your school has a Green Club, join it. If it doesn't, ask if one can be started. As at home, switch off lights when they're not in use, and collect paper, cans and glass for recycling. Walk or cycle to school. Try to use cars less.

Is it true?
You can make a difference.

Yes. Imagine if everyone in your class, your street, even your town recycled things. What a difference that would make!

Sorting trash for recycling

 How can I find out more?

If you would like to help make the Earth a better, safer place to live, now and in the future, you might like to join groups such as Greenpeace, Friends of the Earth or World Wide Fund for Nature. Your library will have their addresses.

Sort your trash for recycling.

249

Glossary

Acid rain Rain that contains chemicals that are harmful to nature.

Active A volcano that is still erupting.

Algae Tiny plants that live in water.

Amber Once liquid tree resin (sap) that has been fossilized.

Amphibian An animal that lives on land and in water, such as a frog.

Asteroid A small rocky body that orbits the Sun.

Astrology Using patterns in the sky as a guide to daily life.

Astronaut Someone who travels into space. The word means "sailor of the stars."

Astronomy The science of space-watching.

Atmosphere The gases or air surrounding a planet.

Axis The imaginary line around which a planet spins.

Bacteria Tiny, living things that live in soil, water and the air.

Bark The tough protective outer layer of a tree, that covers and protects the trunk and the roots.

Big Bang The huge explosion that created the Universe around 15 billion years ago.

Black hole A place in space with such strong gravity that not even light can escape from it.

Blizzard A winter storm with strong winds and heavy snow.

Butte A small, flat-topped hill in the desert.

Capsule A small spacecraft with room for one or two crew.

Carnivore An animal that eats only meat.

Climate The weather conditions in a particular place on Earth.

Comet A body of ice and rock with a long glowing tail that orbits the Sun.

Coniferous Trees which have needle-like leaves and cones, such as cedar, fir and spruce trees.

Constellation The pattern that stars seem to make in the sky, from our viewpoint on Earth.

Core The middle of something.

Cosmology The science of how the Universe (or "cosmos") works.

Cosmonaut A Russian or Soviet astronaut. The word means "sailor of the Universe."

Crust The solid layer of rock on the surface of the Earth, about 5 miles thick under the sea, and 25 miles thick under the continents.

Cumulonimbus Another name for a tall, dark thundercloud.

Cynodont A type of reptile with fur, that evolved into mammals.

Dam A barrier built across a river to stop it flooding or to collect water in a reservoir.

Data Information.

Delta The end of a river where it flows into the sea.

Dinosaur A type of reptile that once lived on Earth, but which has died out.

250

Dormant A sleeping volcano that could erupt at any time.

Drought A time of very dry weather when less rain than normal falls.

Eclipse When light from the Sun or Moon is blocked out. A solar eclipse is when the Moon passes between the Earth and Sun, casting a shadow on the Earth. A lunar eclipse is when Earth passes between the Moon and Sun.

Equator The imaginary line that runs around the middle of the Earth.

Extinct A volcano that has stopped erupting.

Fault A crack in the Earth's crust.

Fold mountain A mountain made when one piece of the Earth's crust crashed into another and pushes up the land in between.

Fossil The remains of an ancient animal or plant preserved in rock.

Fossil fuels Fuels such as coal, oil and natural gas, made from fossilized remains.

Freshwater Water that does not taste salty. Rivers and many lakes are freshwater.

Galaxy A family of star systems that are held together by gravity. Our Solar System is in the Milky Way galaxy.

Genes The instructions that make living things what they are.

Greenhouse gas Gases, such as carbon dioxide or methane, that surround the Earth and keep heat in.

Habitat The surroundings in which an animal or plant lives.

Herbivore An animal that eats only plants.

Lava What magma is called when it erupts from a volcano.

Lens A curved piece of glass.

Lightning conductor A rod on the roof of a tall building that is attached to a strip of metal. It carries electricity from the lightning safely down to the ground.

Magma Rock deep beneath the Earth. It is so hot that it has melted.

Mammal An animal with a backbone that feeds its young on mother's milk.

Mantle The part of the Earth between its crust and its central core.

Meander A large bend in a river. Sometimes a meander gets cut off and forms an oxbow lake.

251

Mesa A large, flat-topped hill in the desert.

Meteorite A space rock that hits the Earth.

Meteoroid A small lump of space rock.

Missile A weapon that is thrown through the air.

Module A section of a space station.

Moon An object in space orbiting a planet.

Nebula A huge cloud of gas and dust where new stars are born.

Nuclear power Power made from radioactive material.

Nutrients Chemicals dissolved in water, used by plants in order to grow.

Observatory A place that houses telescopes and other instruments for viewing the sky.

Omnivore An animal that eats both meat and plants.

Orbit To travel around.

Organic A living thing, or something made from a living thing.

Oxygen A gas that animals breathe in and which keeps them alive.

Payload The cargo that a rocket carries into space.

Peat A dark brown material made from rotten plants.

Planet A body of gas or rock orbiting a star. Planets are not massive enough to be stars. They shine because they reflect the light of the star they are orbiting.

Poles The points at either end of a planet's axis, known as the north and south poles.

Prehistoric An ancient time before writing was invented.

Prey An animal that is killed by another animal for food.

Pulsar A small, dense, fast-spinning neutron star that gives out regular pulses of light and radio waves.

Quasar A region of space giving off more energy than almost any other.

Radioactive A substance that gives off harmful rays and particles.

Reservoirs Lakes used for storing water.

Seasons Different times of the year, when Earth's weather and life change according to the position of the Sun in the sky.

Soil erosion Wearing away of the soil.

Solar panels Mirrors that capture energy from the Sun and turn it into electricity.

Solar power Power made from the Sun.

Solar System Our Sun and everything that travels around it.

Stage A section of a rocket. Rockets usually have three stages.

Stalactite A spike made of stone which grows downward from the ceiling of a cave.

Stalagmite A spike made of stone which grows upward from the floor of a cave.

Star A huge ball of super-hot burning gas.

Submersible An underwater vehicle like a small submarine.

Tarn A small mountain lake carved out by ice millions of years ago.

Telescope An instrument that makes distant objects seem bigger and nearer. They collect light, radio waves, X-rays or other waves.

Twister Another name for a tornado.

Ultraviolet rays Harmful rays from the Sun.

Universe Everything that exists.

Vacuum An empty space with no air.

Wormhole A short cut between two different parts of space.

Index